Ira David Sankey

Male Chorus

Number 2

Ira David Sankey
Male Chorus
Number 2

ISBN/EAN: 9783337334574

Printed in Europe, USA, Canada, Australia, Japan
Cover: Foto ©Thomas Meinert / pixelio.de

More available books at www.hansebooks.com

MALE CHORUS

No. 2.

COMPOSED AND ARRANGED BY

IRA D. SANKEY

AND

GEO. C. STEBBINS.

For use in Christian Associations, Gospel Meetings, and other Religious Services.

Also Department of Secular and Patriotic Songs for Special Occasions.

PREFACE.

With feelings of gratitude for the kindly reception accorded our first **"Male Chorus"** book, we now send forth a second volume.

A few of the most useful and popular Gospel Songs from the former collection have been incorporated in this one, but a large majority of the pieces are entirely new.

To these have been added a fine selection of secular and patriotic pieces for special occasions.

We trust the collection will prove acceptable to all who may have occasion to use it.

IRA D. SANKEY,
GEO. C. STEBBINS.

Male Chorus No. 2.

No. 1.   Praise to the Holy One.

LYMAN E. CUTLER.   IRA D. SANKEY.

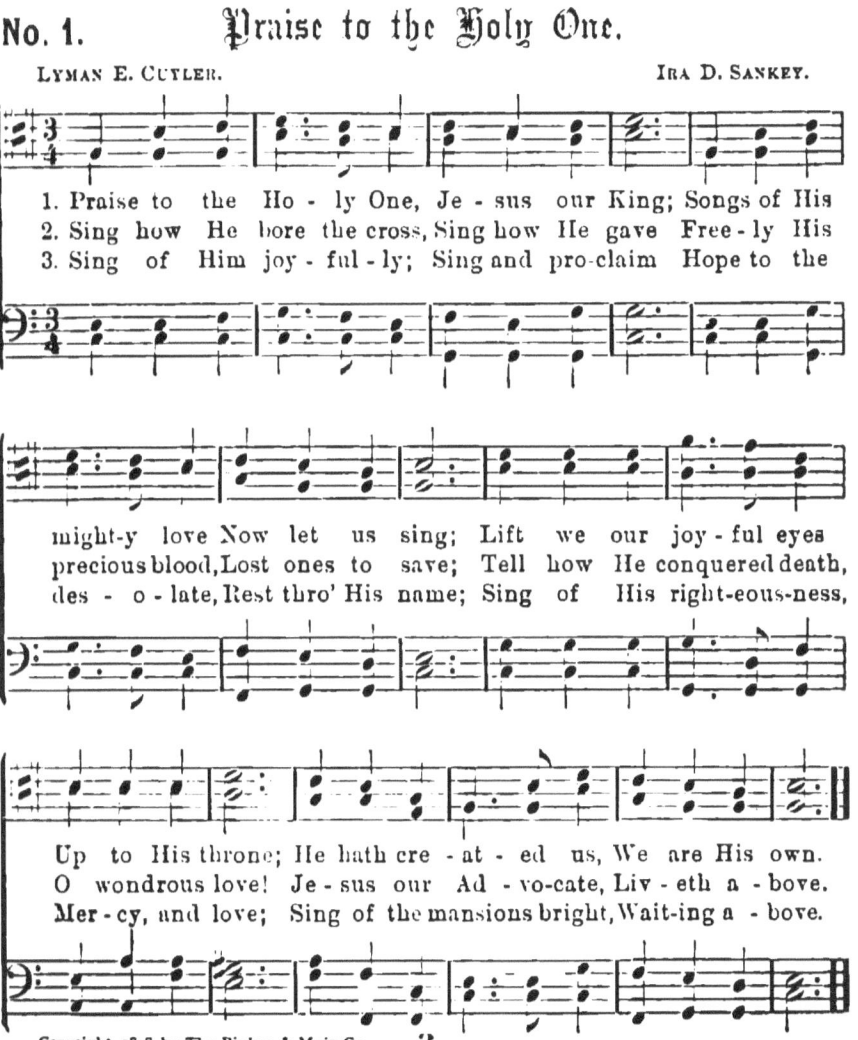

1. Praise to the Holy One, Jesus our King; Songs of His mighty love Now let us sing; Lift we our joyful eyes Up to His throne; He hath created us, We are His own.
2. Sing how He bore the cross, Sing how He gave Freely His precious blood, Lost ones to save; Tell how He conquered death, O wondrous love! Jesus our Advocate, Liveth above.
3. Sing of Him joyfully; Sing and proclaim Hope to the desolate, Rest thro' His name; Sing of His righteousness, Mercy, and love; Sing of the mansions bright, Waiting above.

Copyright, 1898, by The Biglow & Main Co.

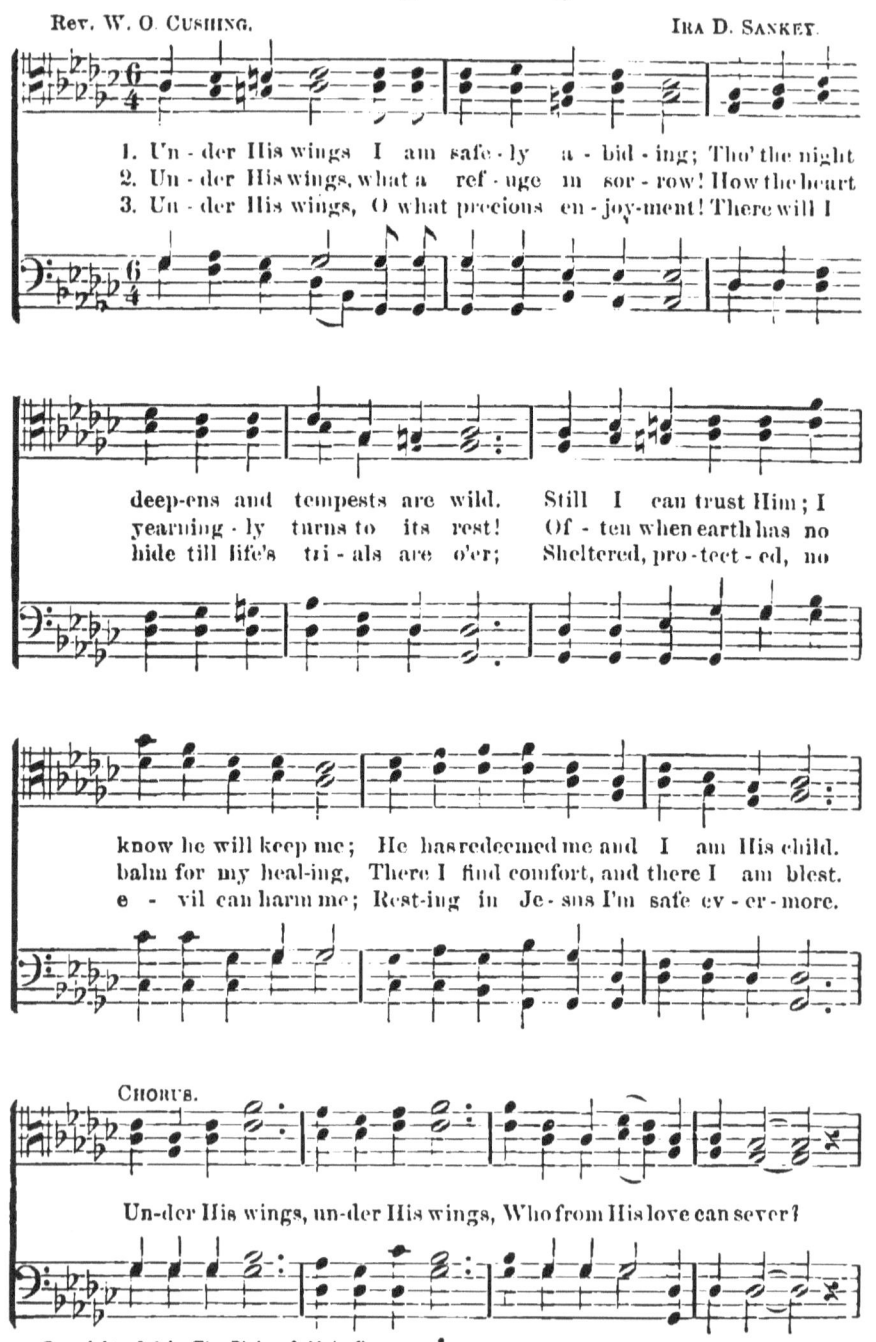

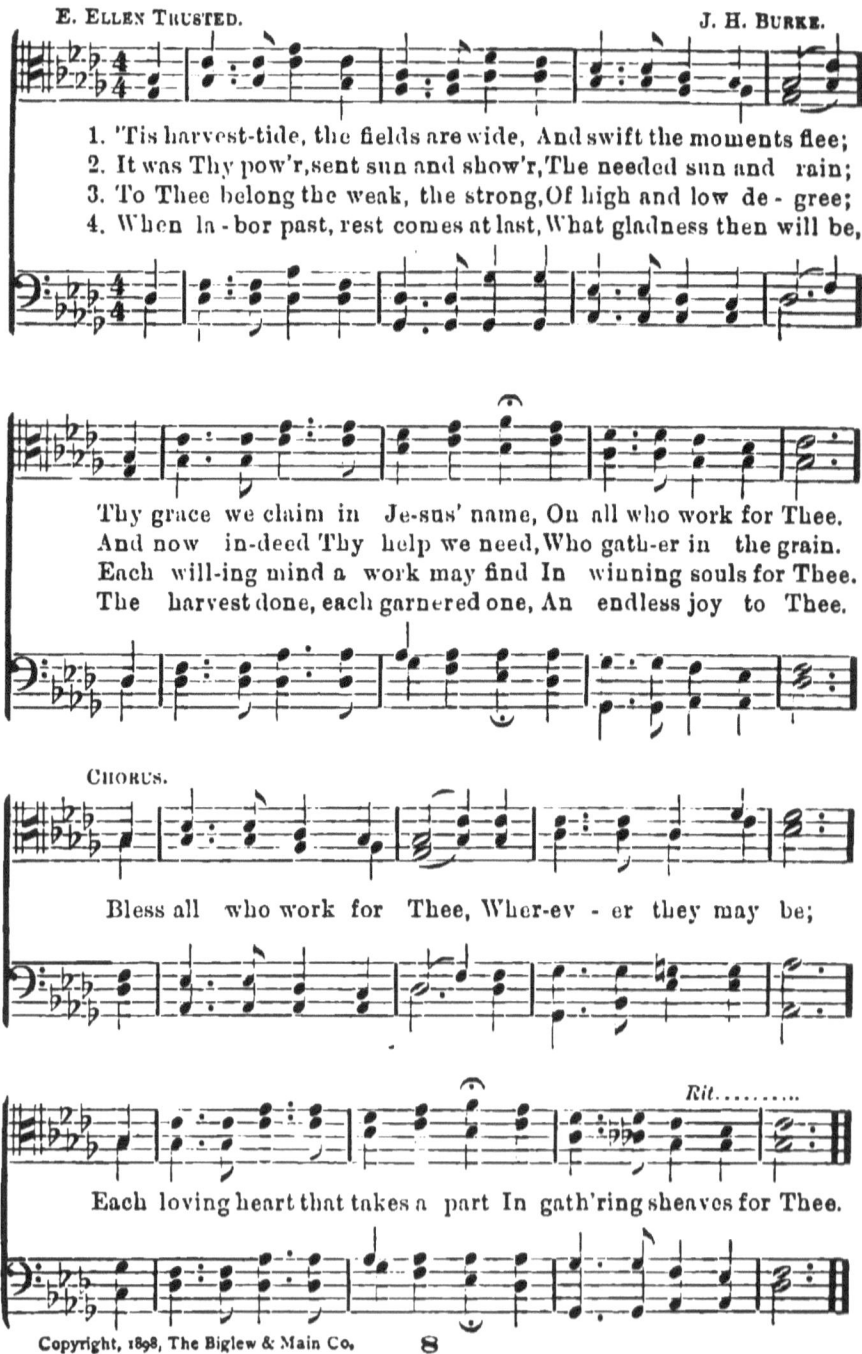

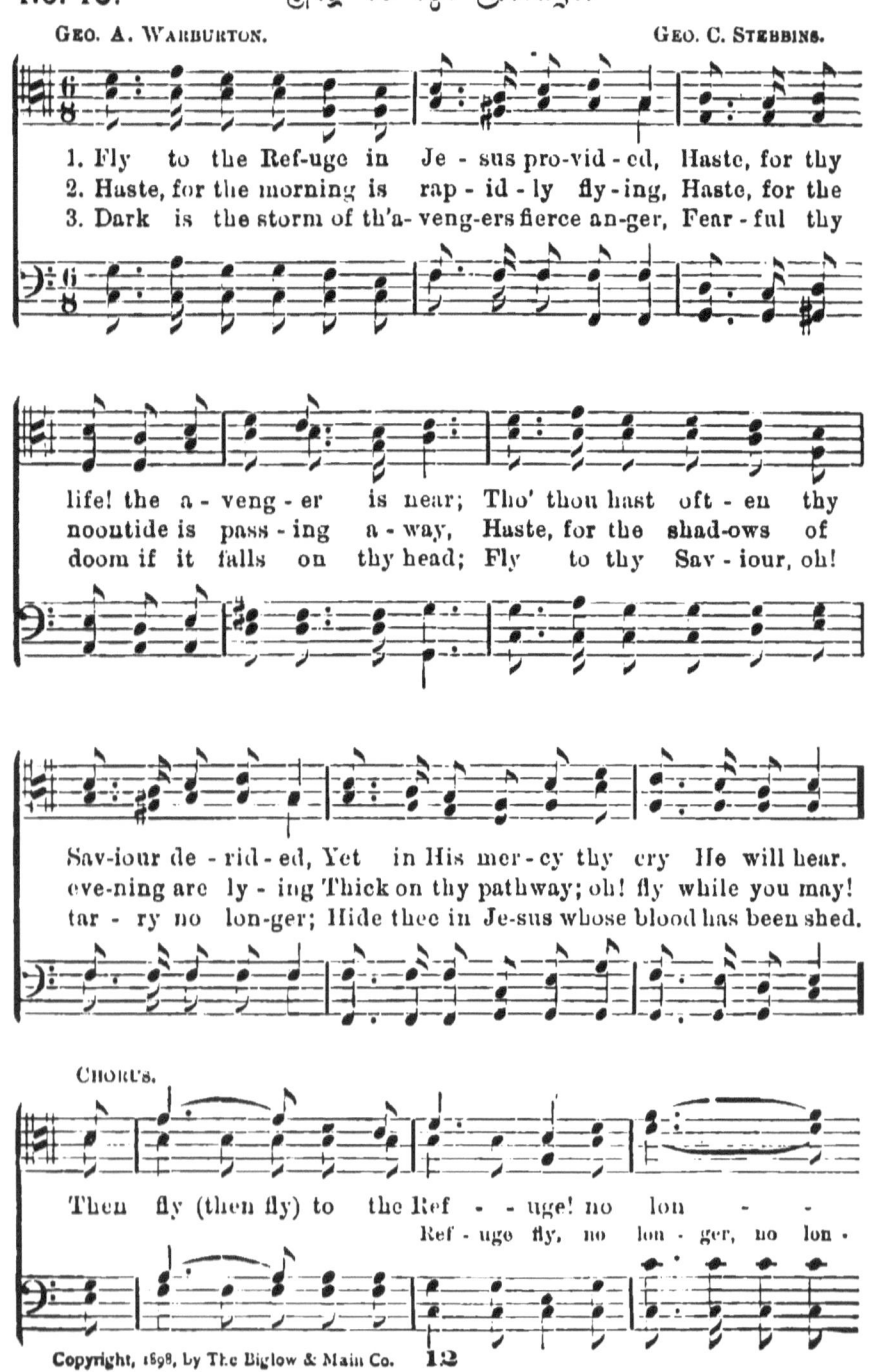

No. 12.   Lead, Kindly Light.

JOHN H. NEWMAN.   JOHN B. DYKES.

1. Lead, kind-ly light, a-mid th'en-circling gloom, Lead Thou me on; The night is dark, and I am far from home, Lead Thou me on; Keep Thou my feet; I do not ask to see The dis-tant scene; one step e-nough for me.

2. I was not ev-er thus, nor prayed that Thou Shouldst lead me on; I loved to choose and see my path; but now Lead Thou me on; I loved the gar-ish day; and, spite of fears, Pride ruled my will; re-mem-ber not past years.

3. So long Thy power hath blest me, sure it still Will lead me on O'er moor and fen, o'er crag and tor-rent, till The night is gone, And with the morn those an-gel fac-es smile, Which I have loved long since, and lost a-while.

Arr. Copyright, 1898, by The Biglow & Main Co.

No. 16. O Paradise!

F. W. Faber.   Joseph Barnby.

1. O Par-a-dise! O Par-a-dise! Who doth not crave for rest?
2. O Par-a-dise! O Par-a-dise! The world is growing old;
3. O Par-a-dise! O Par-a-dise! I great-ly long to see
4. Lord Je-sus, King of Par-a-dise, Oh, keep me in Thy love,

Who would not seek the hap py land Where they that loved are blest?
Who would not be at rest and free Where love is nev-er cold?
The spe-cial place my dearest Lord In love pre-pares for me.
And guide me to that hap py land Of per-fect rest a-bove.

Refrain.

Where loy-al hearts, and true,
Where loy - - al hearts, and true, Stand ever in the light,
All rap-ture thro' and thro,' In God's most ho-ly sight.

Arr. Copyright, 1898, by The Biglow & Main Co.

No. 18. I am Redeemed.

JULIA STERLING.   IRA D. SANKEY.

1. I am redeemed, O praise the Lord; My soul from bondage free,
2. I looked, and lo! from Calvary's Cross A heal-ing fountain stream'd;
3. The debt is paid, my soul is free, And by His mighty pow'r,
4. All glo-ry be to Je-sus' name, I know that He is mine,
5. And when I reach that world more bright Than mortal ev-er dreamed,

Has found 'at last a rest-ing-place In Him who died for me.
It cleansed my heart, and now I sing, Praise God, I am redeemed.
The blood that washed my sins a-way Still cleanseth ev-ery hour.
For on my heart the spir-it seals His pledge of love di-vine.
I'll cast my crown at Je-sus' feet, And cry, "Redeemed, redeemed."

CHORUS.

I am re-deemed (I am re-deemed), I am re-deemed (I am redeemed), I'll sing it o'er and o'er; I am re-

Copyright, 1893, by The Biglow & Main Co.

I am Redeemed.—*Concluded.*

No. 19. ## Only a Little While.

Mrs. M. P. A. Crozier.   Geo. C. Stebbins.

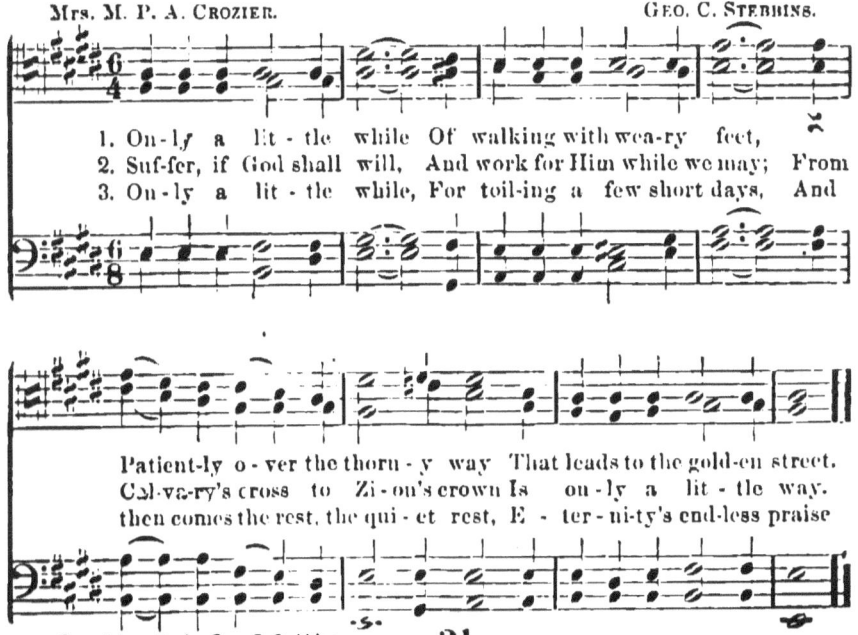

1. On-ly a lit-tle while Of walking with wea-ry feet,
2. Suf-fer, if God shall will, And work for Him while we may; From
3. On-ly a lit-tle while, For toil-ing a few short days, And

Patient-ly o-ver the thorn-y way That leads to the gold-en street.
Cal-va-ry's cross to Zi-on's crown Is on-ly a lit-tle way.
then comes the rest, the qui-et rest, E-ter-ni-ty's end-less praise

Copyright, 1880, by Geo. C. Stebbins.

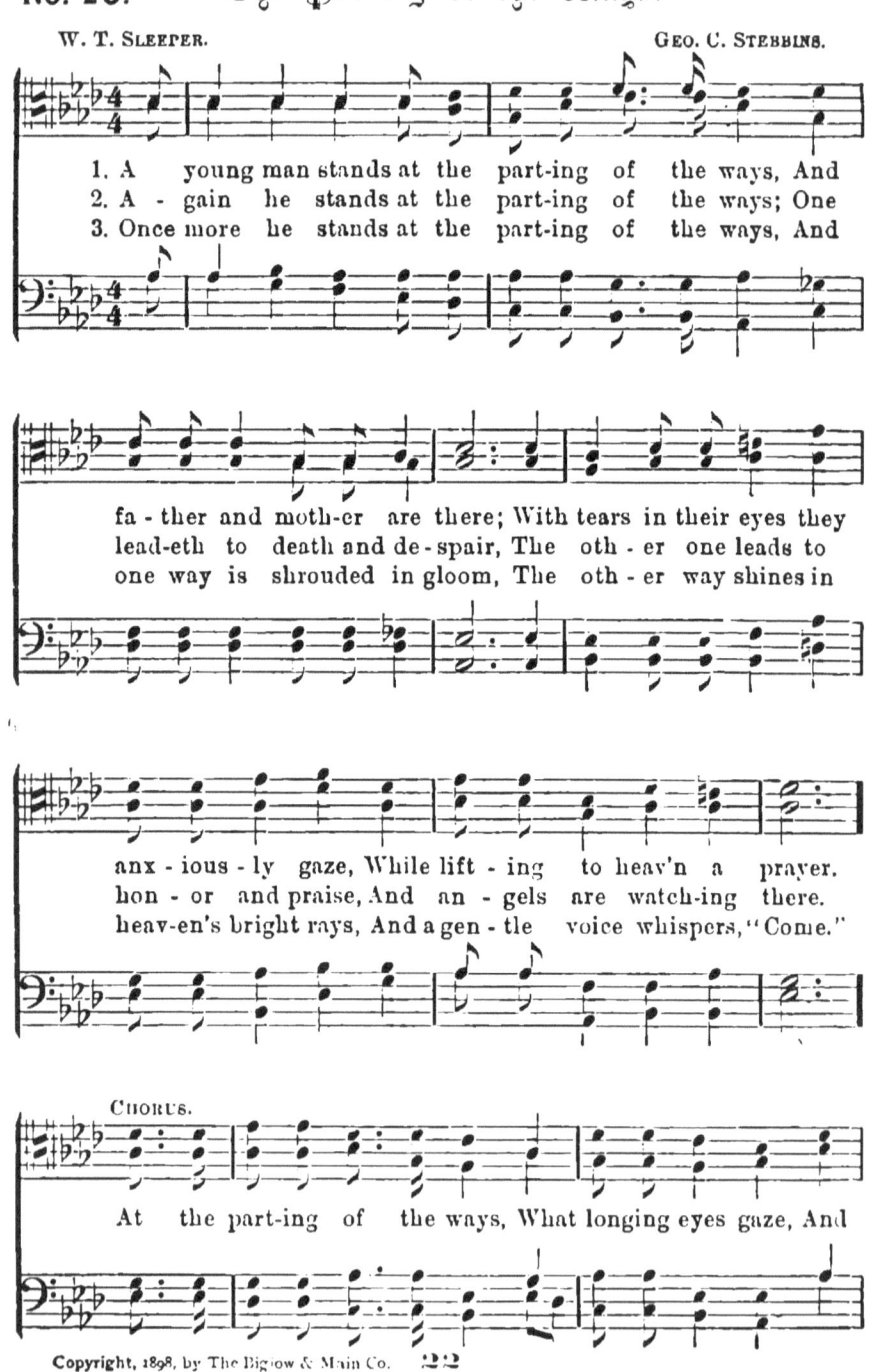

No. 25. Spread the Sails.

F. J. Crosby. Ira D. Sankey.

1. Spread the sails, and speed the ves-sel To   its ha-ven bright and fair;
2. Spread the sails, and speed the ves-sel, There is One who rules the wave;
3. Spread the sails, and speed the ves-sel; Dark at times our voyage may be;
4. Spread the sails, and speed the vessel; Near-er to the port we come;

Je-sus waits to bid us welcome; Our   e-ter-nal rest is there.
And, when billows gath-er round us, His al-might-y arm will save.
But we'll sure-ly make the har-bor; E-ven now its shores we see.
Voic-es hail   us in the dis-tance; Praise the Lord! we're almost home.

CHORUS.

Nev-er-more our faith shall wav-er, Nev-er-more our strength shall fail;

Nev-er-more our hearts be troubled When we anch-or in the vail.

Copyright, 1896, by The Biglow & Main Co.

Come unto Me.—Concluded.

I Heard the Voice of Jesus Say.—Concluded.

I found in Him a rest-ing-place, And He has made me glad.
My thirst was quench'd, my soul reviv'd, And now I live in Him.
And in that Light of Life I'll walk Till traveling days are done.

No. 30. **Show Your Colors.**

Mrs. C. E. Breck. I. H. Meredith, arr.

1. Show your col-ors, while you journey Lift the gos-pel ban-ner high;
2. Plant your col-ors on the mountains, On the hill tops and the plains;
3. 'Neath the col-ors of your Captain Charge against the ranks of sin;

Let it tell of Christ, the Saviour, Who for sinners came to die.
Ral-ly round the glorious standard Of the King who ev-er reigns.
You shall scale the mighty ram-parts, And the vic-t'ry you shall win.

D.S.—*Till it waves o'er ev-'ry na-tion, And the king doms of the world.*

CHORUS.

Show your col-ors, show your col-ors, Let the ban-ner be unfurled,

Copyright, 1896, by The Biglow & Main Co.

No. 32. **O Mother Dear, Jerusalem.**

F. B. P. SAMUEL A. WARD, arr. H. P. M.

1. O Mother dear, Jerusalem, When shall I come to thee?
2. No dimming cloud o'ershadows thee, Nor gloom, nor darksome night;
3. Right thro' thy streets with pleasing sound The flood of life doth flow,

When shall my sorrows have an end? Thy joys when shall I see?
But ev-'ry soul shines as the sun, For God himself gives light.
And on the banks, on either side, The trees of life do grow.

O happy harbor of God's saints, O sweet and pleasant soil!
Thy walls are made of precious stone, Thy bulwarks diamond square;
Those trees each month yield ripened fruit; For evermore they spring;

In thee no sorrow can be found, Nor grief, nor care, nor toil.
Thy gates are all of orient pearl: O God, if I were there!
And all the nations of the earth To Thee their honors bring.

Arr. Copyright, 1898, by The Biglow & Main Co. Used by permission.

No. 33. "All's Clear up Aloft."

A heavy fog had settled on the river Clyde. The passengers on a steamer became apprehensive at the rate of speed maintained. At length they went forward and remonstrated with the captain on the bridge. He replied, "All's clear up aloft; the fog is only on the surface; there is no danger."

D. W. Whittle.   Geo. C. Stebbins.

1. "All's clear up a-loft," said the cap-tain true, As fear-less-ly on-ward we sped, "No fog is up here, it is all be-low, The sun shines just o-ver our head."
2. "All's clear up a-loft," for the Lord, our Light, Our Strength and our Ref-uge and Song, Is there in command thro' the day and night, Our Cap-tain so true and so strong.
3. "All's clear up a-loft," all is safe be-low, Tho' fogs and tho' mists may pre-vail; With eye all undimm'd stands the Captain true, To guide us as on-ward we sail.
4. "All's clear up a-loft," for, with Him on high, The dark is the same as the light; He knows all the per-il and dan-gers nigh, His beacon shines on in the night.
5. "All's clear up a-loft;" with the Capt-ain true, Our course and our speed will be right; We'll trust without fear, for the One we know Is there up a-loft in the light.

Chorus.

"All's clear up a-loft;" O glad words of cheer! O Captain so true and so brave! "All's clear up a—

Copyright 1898, by The Biglow & Main Co.

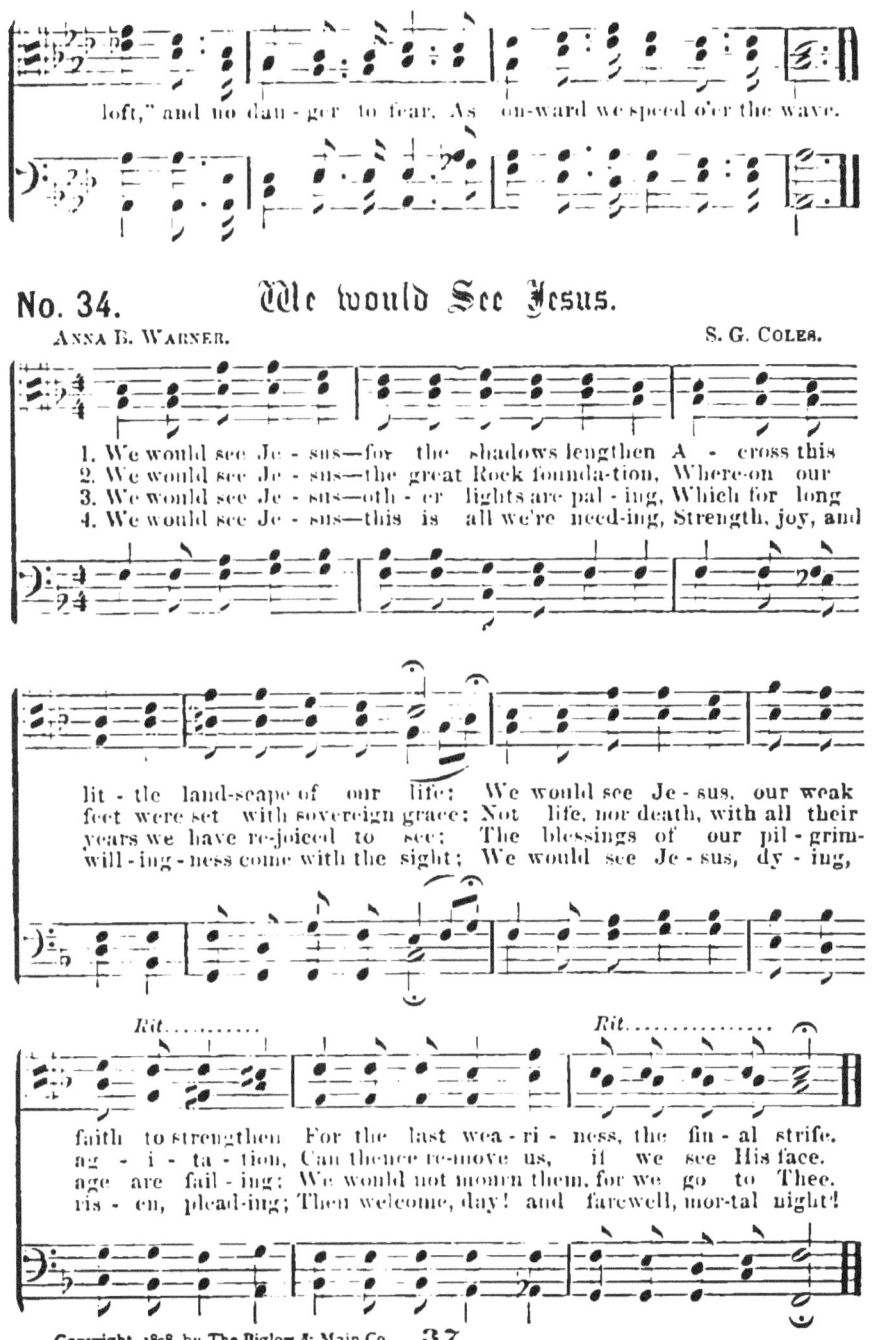

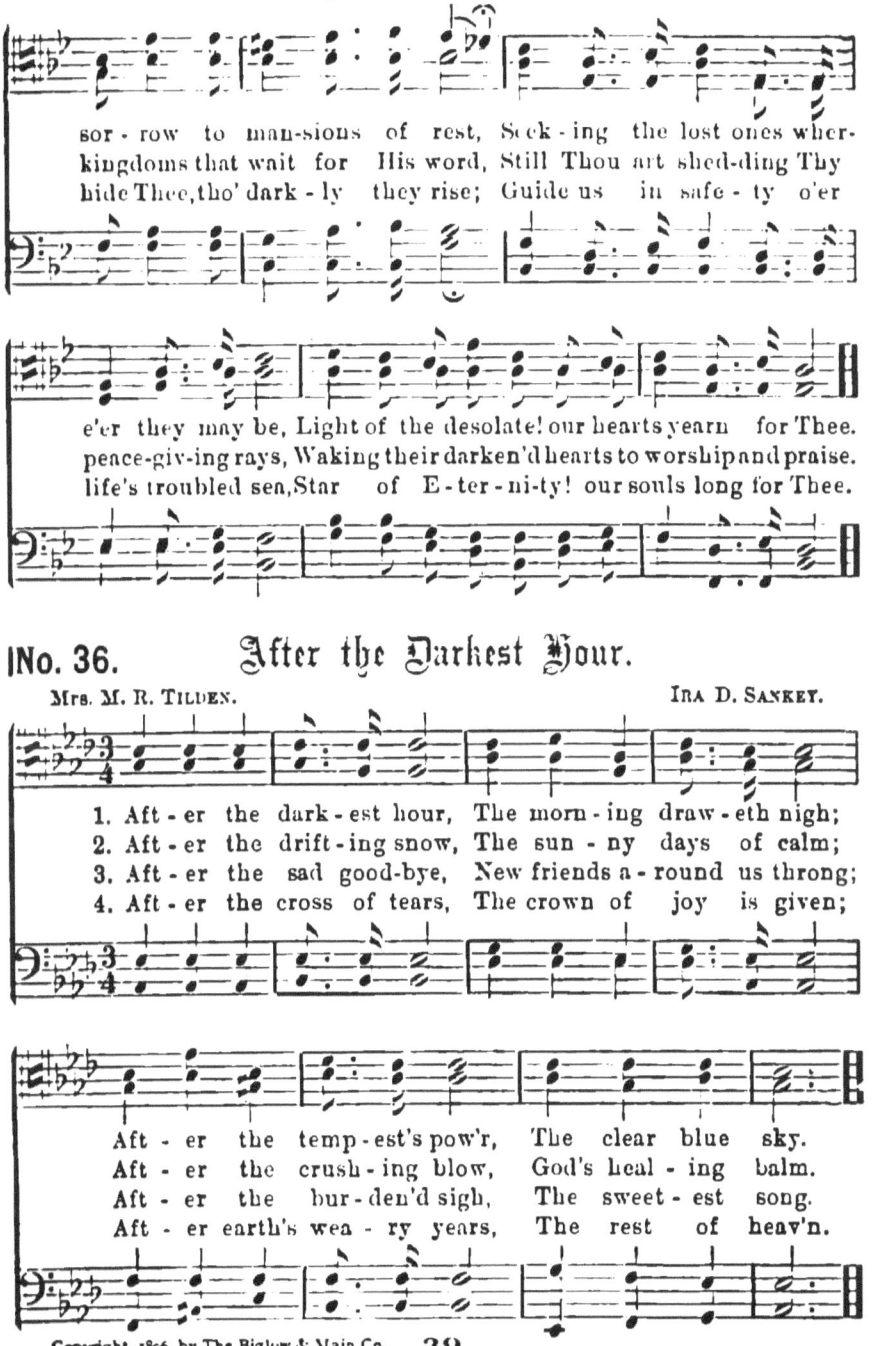

Sweet Peace.—Concluded.

wonderful, wonderful peace, Sweet peace, the gift of God's love.

No. 38. Remember Me, O Mighty One!

Anon.
JOANNA KINKEL, arr.

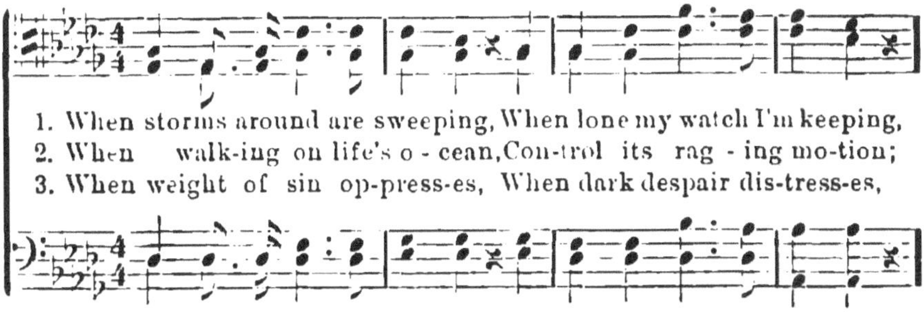

1. When storms around are sweeping, When lone my watch I'm keeping,
2. When walk-ing on life's o - cean, Con-trol its rag - ing mo-tion;
3. When weight of sin op-press-es, When dark despair dis-tress-es,

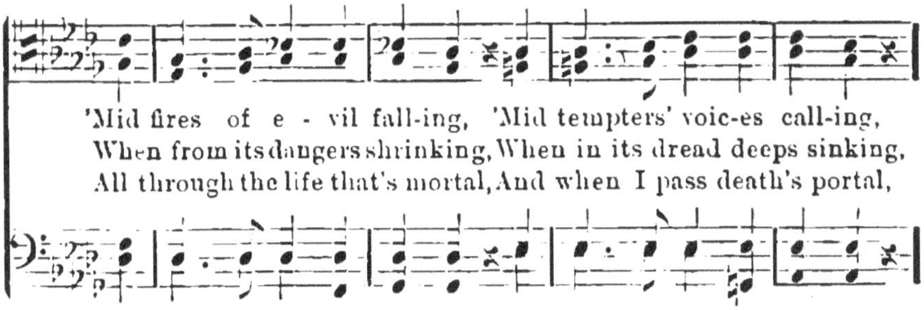

'Mid fires of e - vil fall-ing, 'Mid tempters' voic-es call-ing,
When from its dangers shrinking, When in its dread deeps sinking,
All through the life that's mortal, And when I pass death's portal,

CHORUS.

Re - member me, O Mighty One! Remember me, O Mighty One!

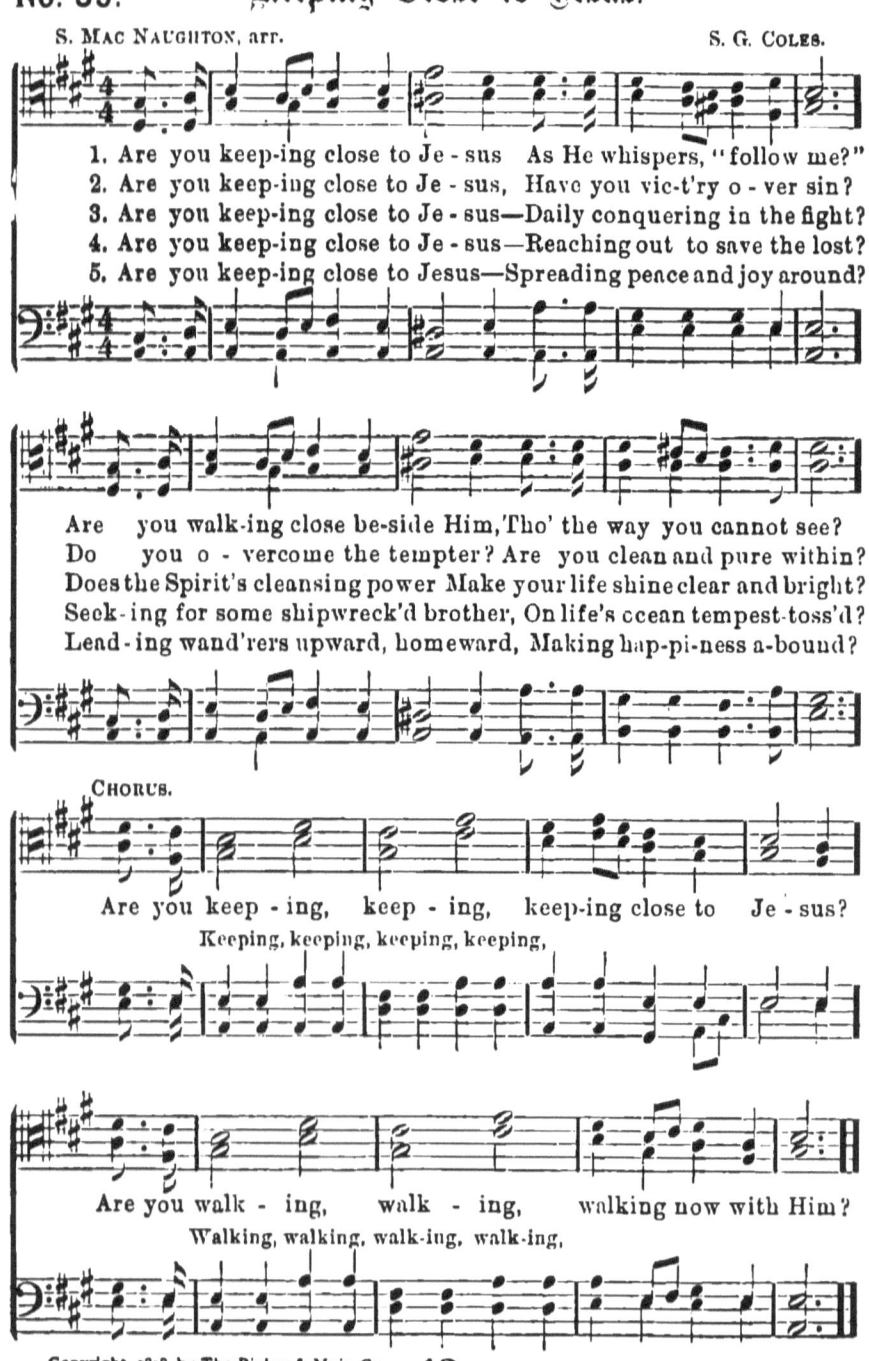

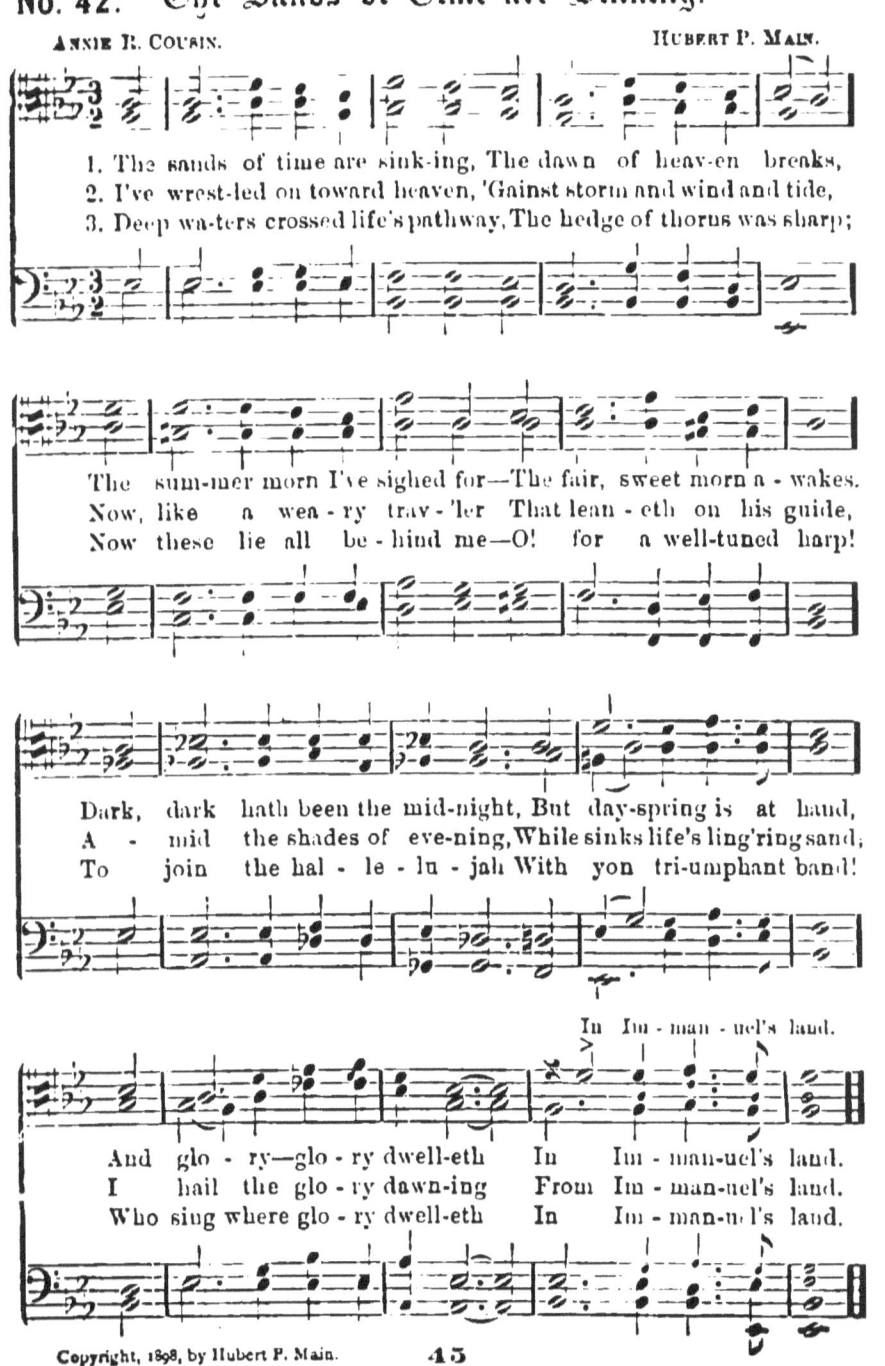

No. 44. Rock of Ages.

A. M. TOPLADY.   GEO. C. STEBBINS.

1. Rock of A - - ges, cleft for me,   Let me
2. Not the la - - bor of my hands,   Can ful -
3. Noth-ing in   my hands I bring,   Sim - ply
4. While I draw   this fleet-ing breath, When mine

1. Rock of A - - ges, cleft for me,
2. Not the la - bor   of my hands
3. Noth-ing in   my   hands I bring,
4. While I draw this fleet - ing breath,

hide   my-self in Thee;   Let the wa - - ter and the
fil   Thy law's demands;   Could my zeal   no re - spite
to   Thy cross I cling;   Nak-ed, come   to Thee for
eyes   shall close in death, When I soar   to worlds un-

Let me hide my - self in Thee;   Let the wa - ter
Can ful - fil Thy law's de-mands;   Could my zeal no
Sim - ply to Thy cross I cling;   Naked, come to
When mine eyes shall close in death, When I soar to

Copyright, 1898, by The Biglow & Main Co.   47

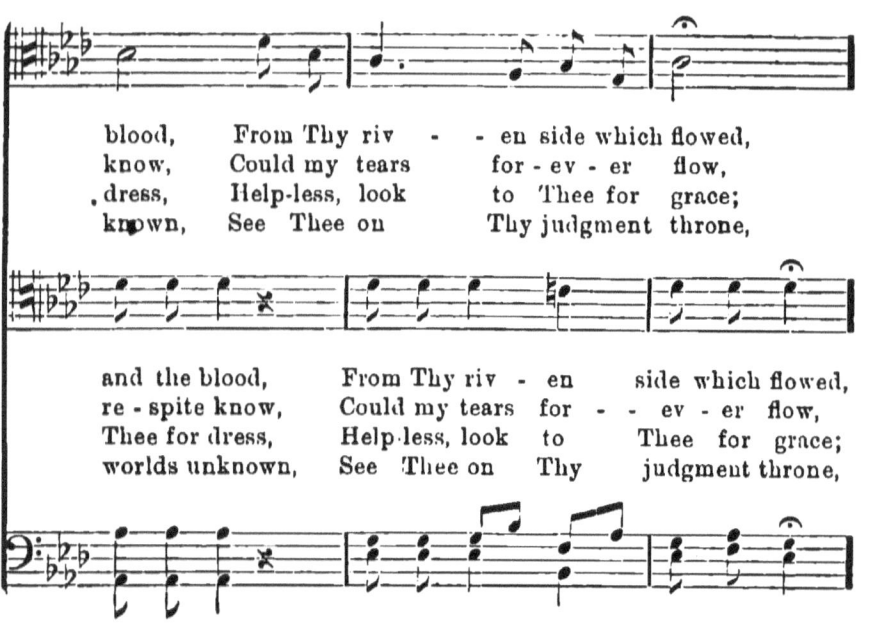

Rock of Ages.—*Concluded.*

from its guilt and power; Be of sin the doub-le
save, and Thou a-lone; All for sin could not a-
Sav - iour, or I die; Foul, I to the fount-ain
hide my-self in Thee; Rock of A - - ges, cleft for

Save me from its guilt and power; Be of sin the
Thou must save, and Thou a - lone; All for sin could
Wash me, Saviour, or I die; Foul, I to the
Let me hide my - self in Thee; Rock of A - ges,

Rit...............

cure, Save me from its guilt and power.
tone; Thou must save, and Thou a - lone.
fly, Wash me, Sav - - iour, or I die.
me, Let me hide my - self in Thee.

doub-le cure, Save me from its guilt and power.
not a - tone; Thou must save, and Thou a - lone.
fountain fly, Wash me, Sav - iour, or I die.
cleft for me, Let me hide my - self in Thee.

49

3 Time is now fleeting, the moments are passing,
Passing from you and from me;
Shadows are gathering, death-beds are coming,
Coming for you and for me.

4 Oh, for the wonderful love He has promis'd,
Promised for you and for me;
Though we have sinned He has mercy and pardon,
Pardon for you and for me.

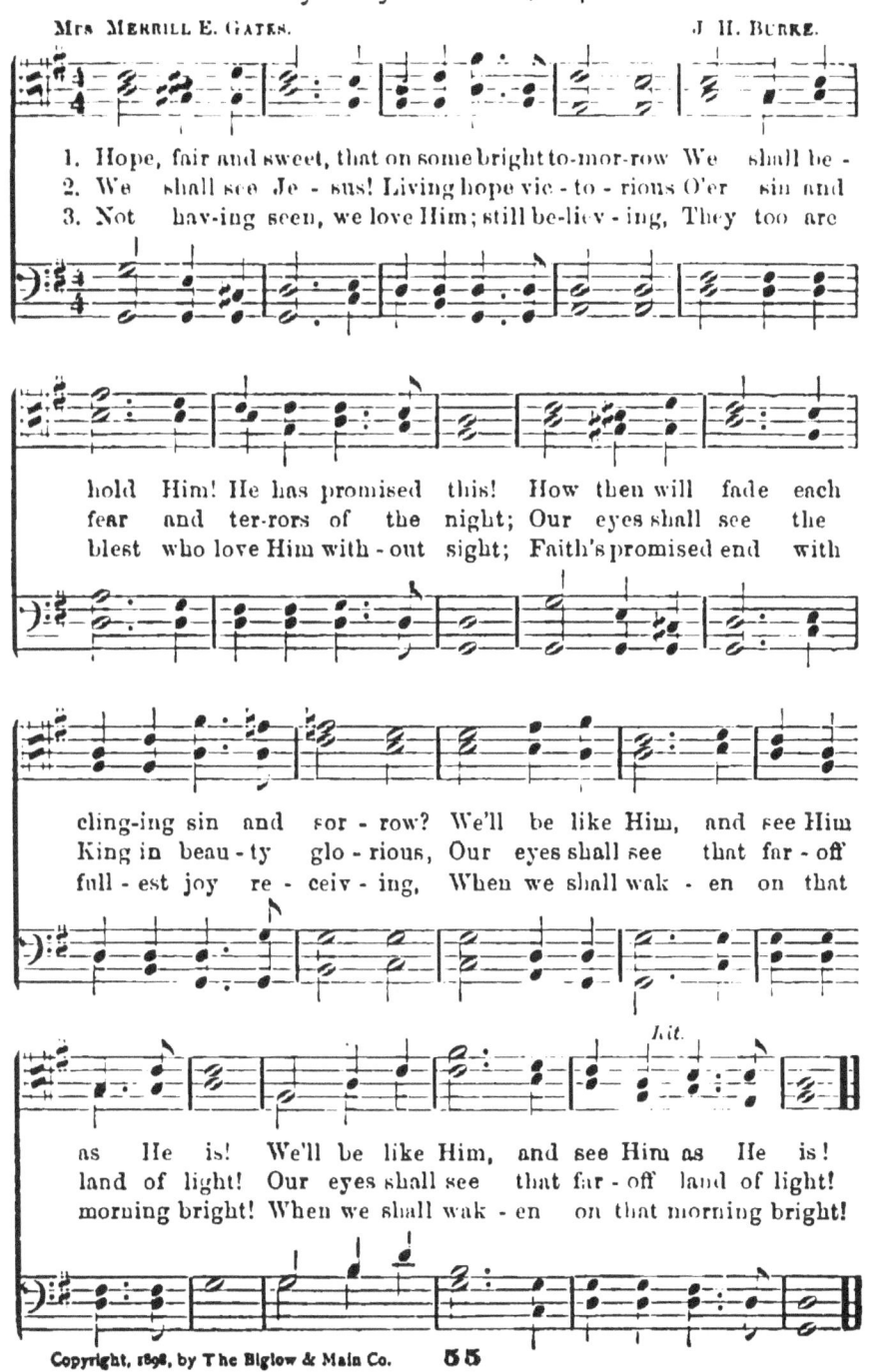

The Shepherd True.—*Concluded.*

No. 56. The Christian's Good-night.

SARAH DOUDNEY.   IRA D. SANKEY.

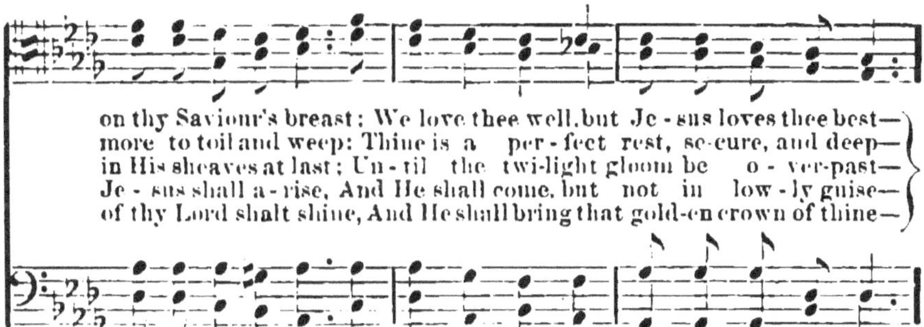

1. Sleep on, be-lov-ed, sleep, and take thy rest; Lay down thy head up-on thy Saviour's breast: We love thee well, but Je-sus loves thee best—
2. Calm is thy slum-ber as an infant's sleep: But thou shalt wake no more to toil and weep: Thine is a per-fect rest, se-cure, and deep—
3. Un-til the shadows from the earth are cast: Un-til He gath-ers in His sheaves at last; Un-til the twi-light gloom be o-ver-past—
4. Un-til the East-er glo-ry lights the skies; Un-til the dead in Je-sus shall a-rise, And He shall come, but not in low-ly guise—
5. Un-til made beau-ti-ful by Love divine, Thou, in the like-ness of thy Lord shalt shine, And He shall bring that gold-en crown of thine—

Good-night! Good-night! Good-night!

6 Only "good-night," beloved—not
   "farewell!"   [dwell
A little while, and all His saints shall
In hallowed union, indivisible—
   Good-night!

7 Until we meet again before His throne,
Clothed in the spotless robe He gives
   His own,
Until we know even as we are known—
   Good-night!

Copyright, 1888, by Ira D. Sankey.

Blue Galilee.—Concluded.

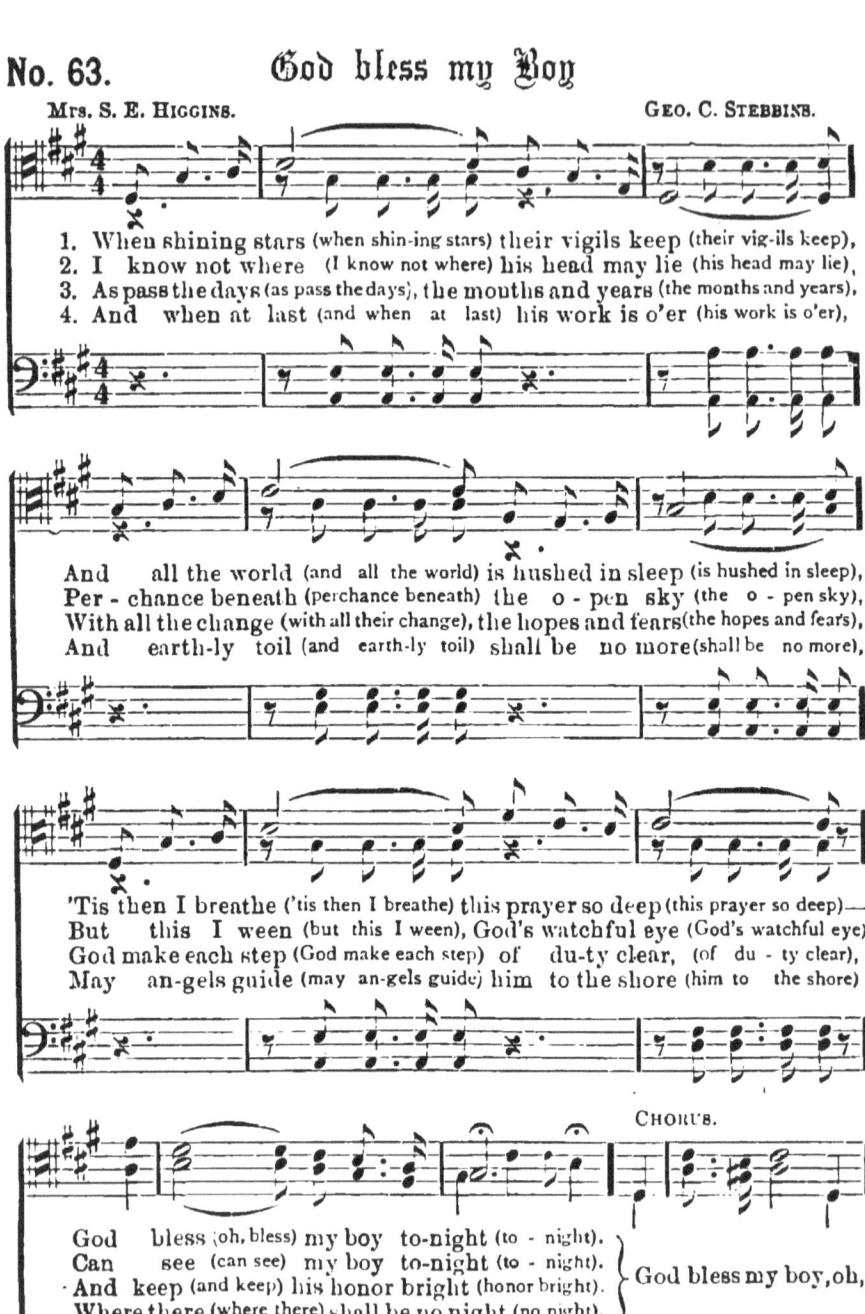

Onward and Upward.—Concluded.

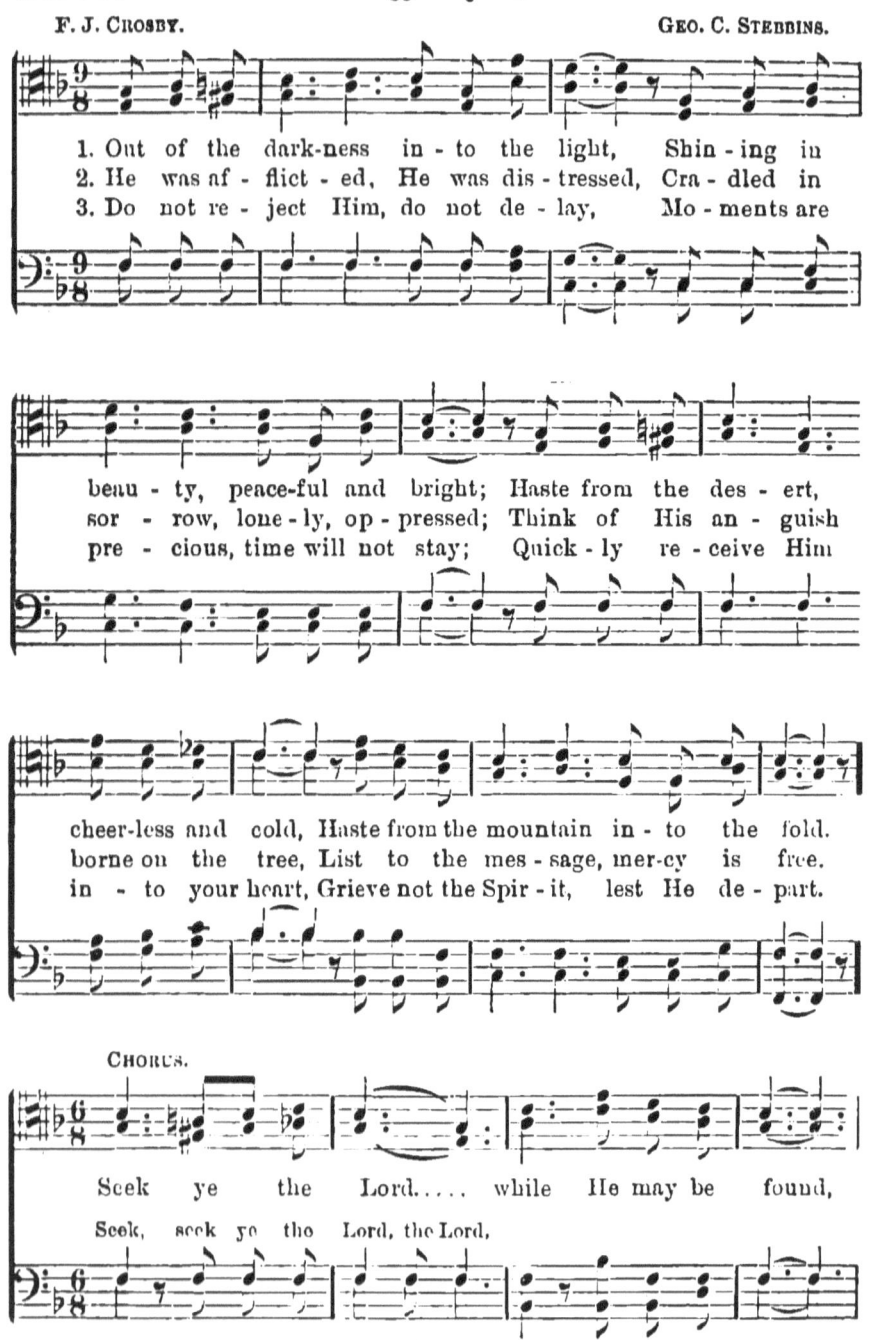

Seek Ye the Lord.—_Concluded._

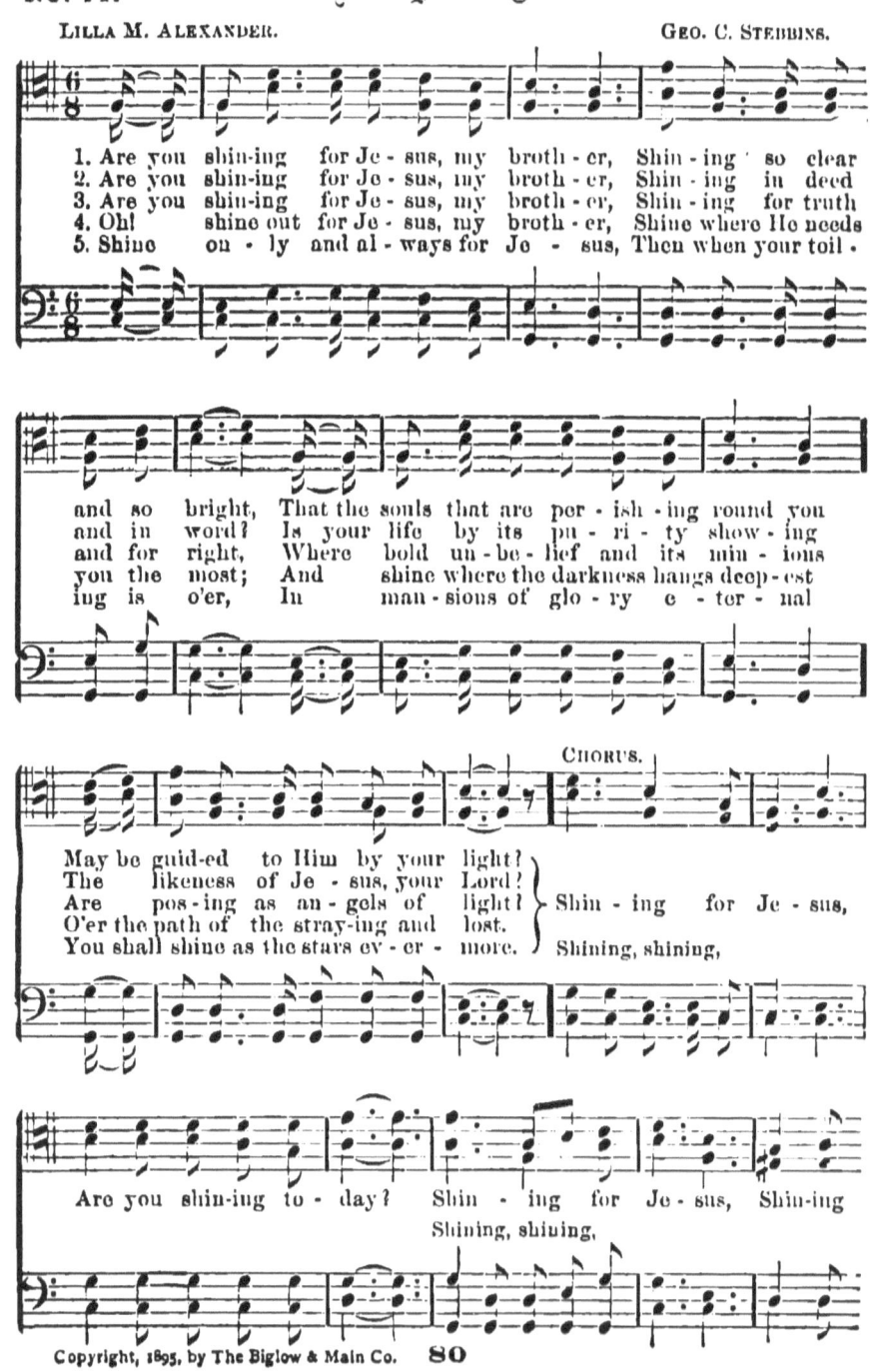

Shining for Jesus. — *Concluded.*

all the way. Shin-ing for Je-sus In this world of
Shin-ing, shin-ing,

care; Shin-ing for Je-sus, Shin-ing ev-ery-where.
Shin-ing, shin-ing,

No. 72. **He is Despised.**

Isa. 53:3–6.   Geo. C. Stebbins.

1. "He is despised and re - - - - - - jected of men;
2. And we hid as it were our.................. fac - es from him;
3. Surely he hath borne our griefs, and............ carried our sorrows;
4. But he was wounded for our transgressions, he } our in-iquities:
    was bruised for........................
5. All we like sheep, have gone astray; we have } his own way;
    turned every one to.....................

A man of sorrows,............... and ac-quainted with grief:
He was despised, and.......... we es-teemed him not.
Yet we did esteem him stricken, } God, — and af-flicted.
    smitten of......................
The chastisment of our peace was } stripes— we are healed.
    upon him; and with his.......
And the Lord hath laid on him } iqui-ty of us all." A-men.
    the in - - - - -

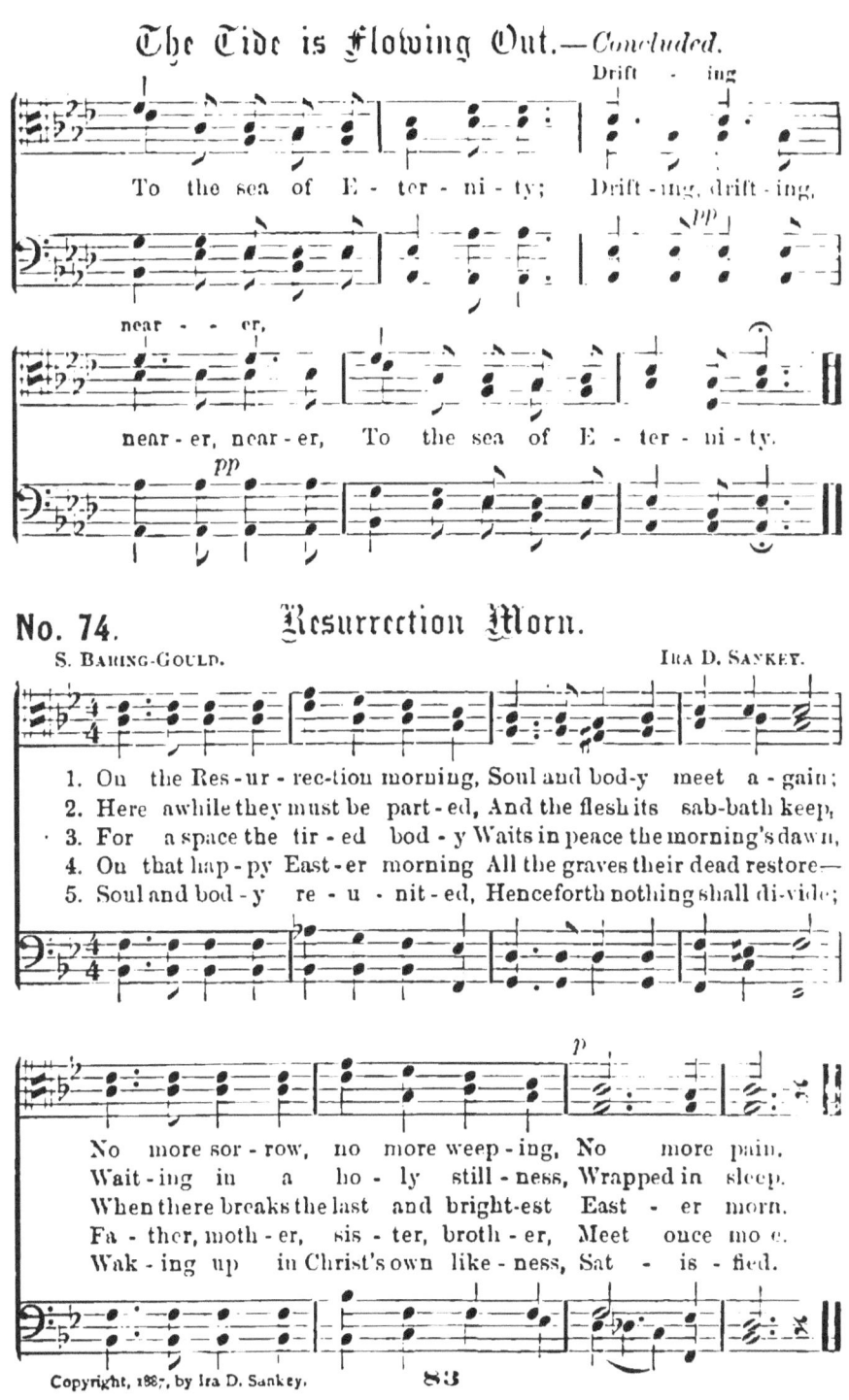

One Sweetly Solemn Thought.—Concluded.

God shall Wipe away all Tears.—Continued.

God shall Wipe away all Tears.—Concluded.

I Have Enough.—*Concluded.*

so di-vine (so divine), I have e-nough for-ev-er.
I have

No. 83. **Hark! There comes a Whisper.**

F. J. CROSBY.   W. H. DOANE, by per.

1. Hark! there comes a whis-per Steal-ing on thine ear: 'Tis the Saviour
2. With that voice so gen-tle, Dost thou hear Him say: "Tell Me all thy
3. Wouldst thou find a Ref-uge For thy soul oppressed? Je-sus kind-ly
4. At the cross of Je-sus Let thy bur-den fall, While He gently

REFRAIN.

call-ing, Soft, soft and clear.
sor-rows; Come, come a-way!"
answers: "I am thy Rest."
whispers. "I'll bear it all."

"Give thy heart to me, Once I

to me,

died for thee;" Hark! Hark! thy Saviour calls: Come, sinner, come!
for thee;

Copyright, 1888, by W. H. Doane.

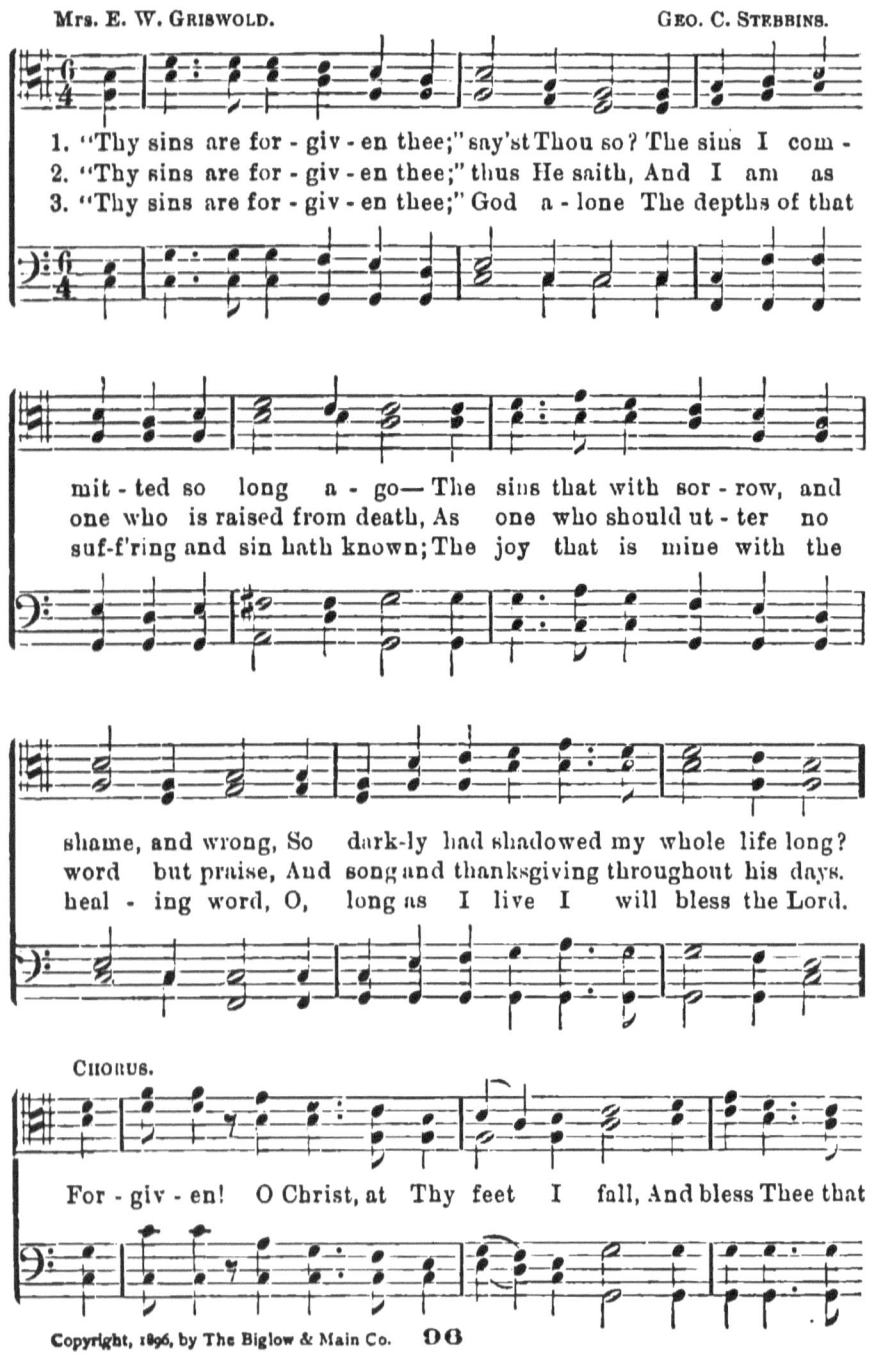

No. 88. Praise and Magnify Our King.

L. EDWARDS.   JNO. R. SWENEY.

1. Great is the Lord, who rul-eth o-ver all! Wake, wake and sing,
2. Great is the Lord, who spake and it was done; Wake, wake and sing,
3. Great is the Lord, and ho-ly is His name! Wake, wake and sing,

wake, wake and sing; Down at His feet in ad-o-ra-tion fall,
wake, wake and sing; Hon-or and strength, do-min-ion He has won,
wake, wake and sing; An-gels and men His wondrous works pro-claim,

CHORUS.

Praise and mag-ni-fy our King. }
Praise and mag-ni-fy our King. } { O ye redeemed a-bove,
Praise and mag-ni-fy our King. }   Strike, strike your harps of love,

Hail the blessed One, hail the Mighty One; Sweetly His wonders tell,

Loud-ly His glo-ry swell, Praise and mag-ni-fy our King.

Used by permission, J. R. S.

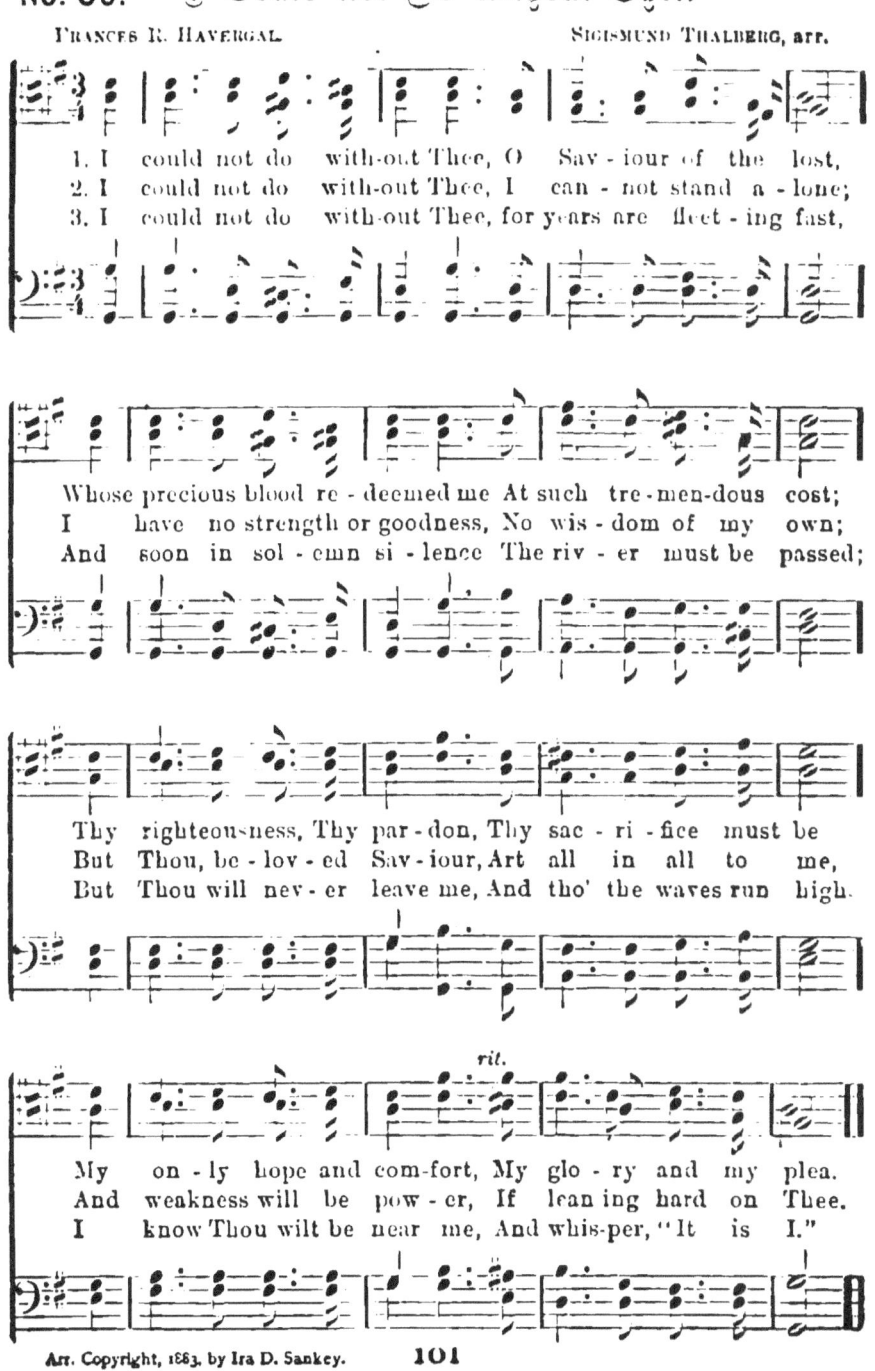

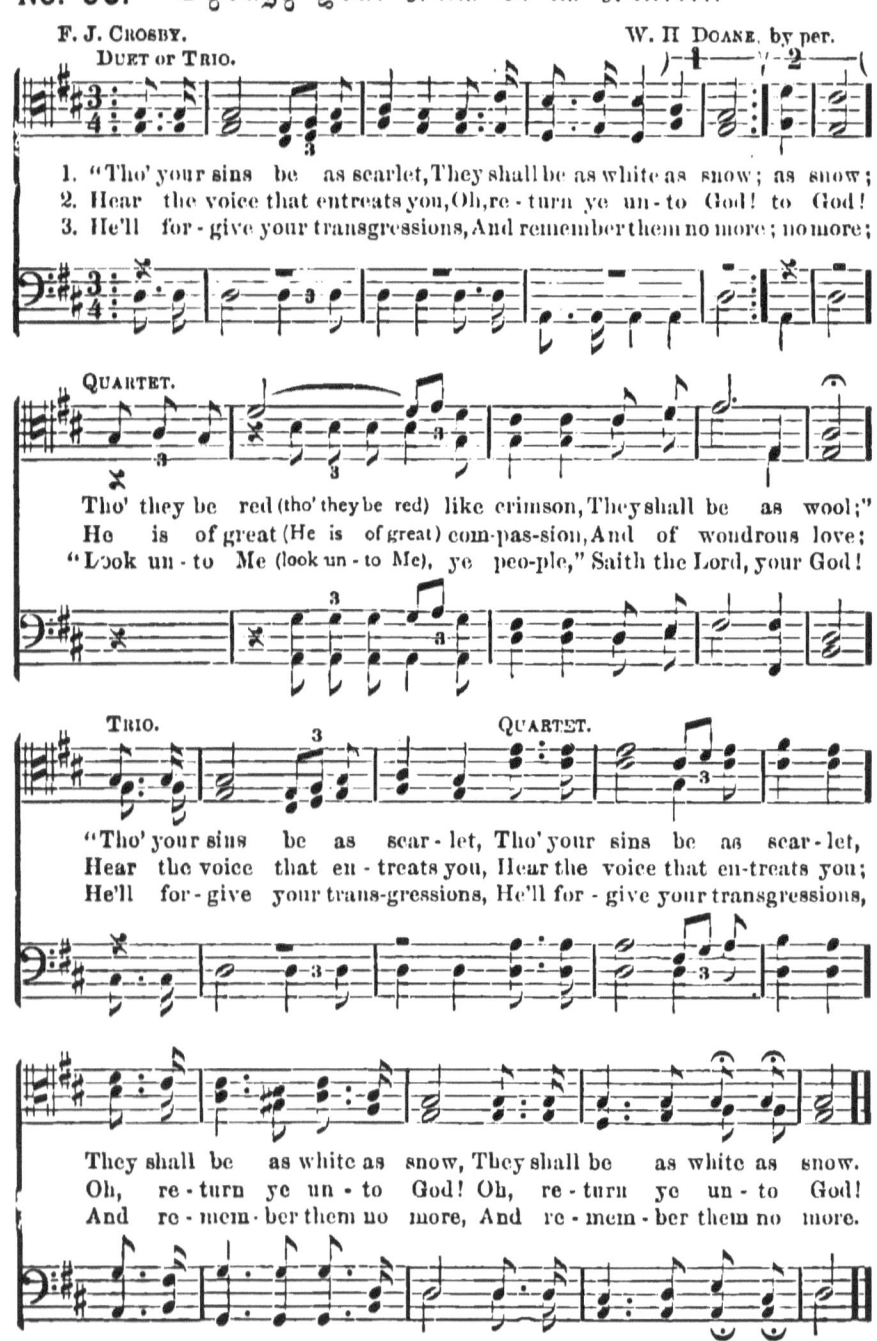

No. 91. **Day is Dying in the West.**

MARY A. LATHBURY.   WM. F. SHERWIN.
Melody in 2d Tenor.

1. Day is dy-ing in the west; Heav'n is touching earth with rest:
2. Lord of life, be-neath the dome Of the u - ni-verse, Thy home;
3. While the deep'ning shadows fall, Heart of Love, en - fold-ing all,
4. When for-ev - er from our sight, Pass the stars— the day—the night,

Wait and wor-ship while the night Sets her eve-ning lamps a-light Thro'
Gath - er us, who seek Thy face To the fold of Thy embrace, For
Thro' the glo - ry and the grace, Of the stars that veil Thy face, Our
Lord of an - gels, on our eyes Let e - ter - nal morn-ing rise, And

CHORUS.

all the sky. ⎫
Thou art high. ⎬ Ho-ly, ho-ly, ho - ly, Lord God of hosts! Heav'n and
hearts as - cend. ⎪
shad-ows end. ⎭

earth are full of Thee! Heav'n and earth are praising Thee, O Lord most high!

Copyright, 1877, by J. H. Vincent. Used by per.

SECULAR AND PATRIOTIC SONGS

FOR

SPECIAL OCCASIONS.

No. 93.   *America.*

SAMUEL F. SMITH, D.D.   Adapted by HENRY CAREY.

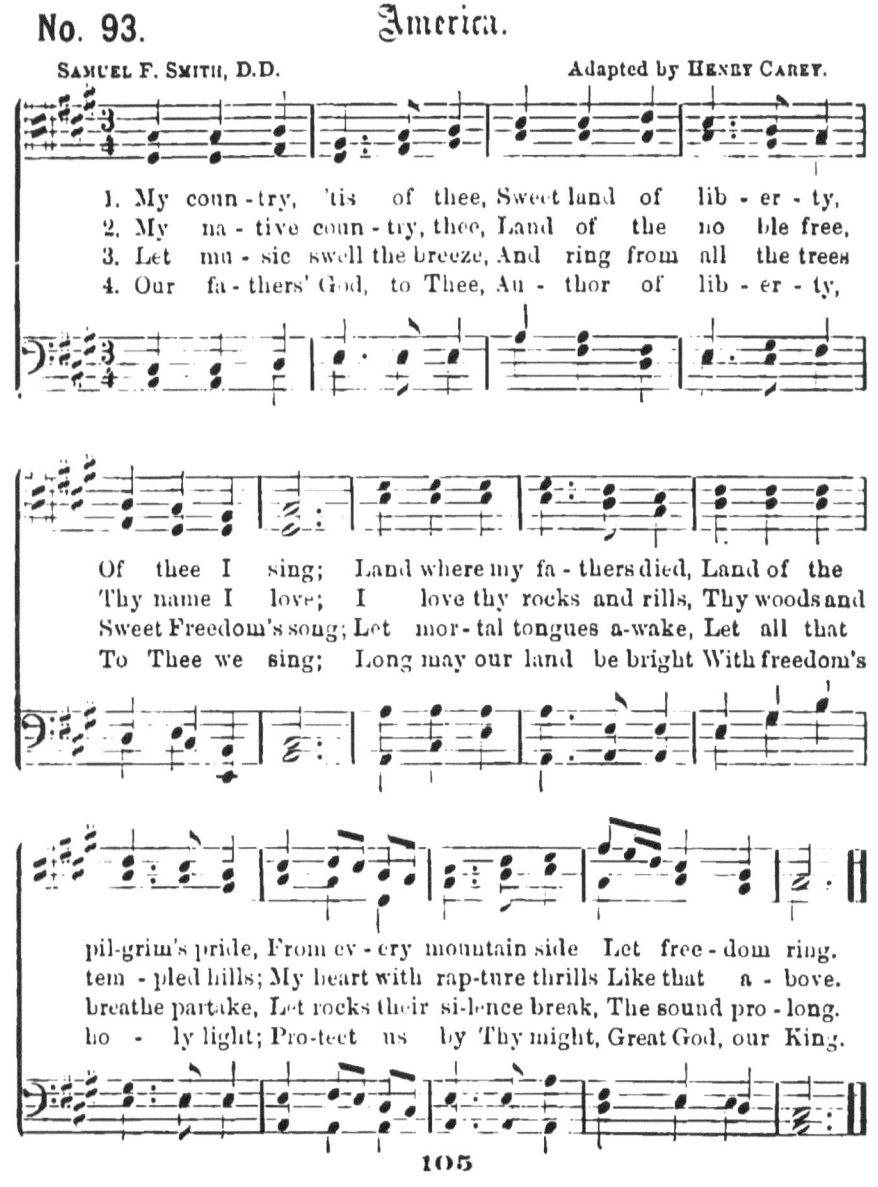

1. My coun-try, 'tis of thee, Sweet land of lib-er-ty,
2. My na-tive coun-try, thee, Land of the no-ble free,
3. Let mu-sic swell the breeze, And ring from all the trees
4. Our fa-thers' God, to Thee, Au-thor of lib-er-ty,

Of thee I sing; Land where my fa-thers died, Land of the
Thy name I love; I love thy rocks and rills, Thy woods and
Sweet Freedom's song; Let mor-tal tongues a-wake, Let all that
To Thee we sing; Long may our land be bright With freedom's

pil-grim's pride, From ev-ery mountain side Let free-dom ring.
tem-pled hills; My heart with rap-ture thrills Like that a-bove.
breathe partake, Let rocks their si-lence break, The sound pro-long.
ho-ly light; Pro-tect us by Thy might, Great God, our King.

The Star-Spangled Banner.—*Concluded.*

bombs burst-ing in air, Gave proof thro' the night that our flag was still there; Oh, say, does the Star-spangled Ban-ner yet wave O'er the land of the free and the home of the brave?

of the morn-ing's first beam, In full glo-ry re-flect-ed, now shines on the stream: 'Tis the Star-spangled Banner: Oh, long may it wave O'er the land of the free and the home of the brave.

3 And where is that band who so vauntingly swore,
    That the havoc of war and the battles confusion,
A home and a country should leave us no more?
    Their blood has washed out their foul footsteps' pollution.
No refuge could save the hireling and slave
    From the terror of flight or the gloom of the grave:
And the Star-spangled Banner in triumph doth wave
    O'er the land of the free and the home of the brave.

4 Oh, thus be it ever when freeman shall stand
    Between their loved homes and the war's desolation;
Blest with victory and peace, may the heaven-rescued land
    Praise the Power that hath made and preserved us a nation!
Then conquer we must, when our cause it is just,
    And this be our motto: "In God is our trust!"
And the Star-spangled Banner in triumph shall wave
    O'er the land of the free and the home of the brave.

No. 95.   **Hail! Columbia.**

JOSEPH HOPKINSON.   J. FEYLES.

1. Hail! Co-lum-bia, hap-py land,   Hail! ye he-roes, heav'n-born band, Who fought and bled in Freedom's cause, Who fought and bled in Freedom's cause, And, when the storm of war was gone, En-joyed the peace your val-or won! Let In-de-pen-dence

2. Im-mor-tal pat-riots, rise once more, De-fend your rights, de-fend your shore, Let no rude foe with impious hand, Let no rude foe with impious hand, In-vade the shrine where sacred lies, Of toil and blood the well-earned prize, While of-f'ring peace, sin-

108

Hail! Columbia.—*Concluded.*

be our boast, Ev - er mind-ful what it cost, Ev - er grate-ful for the prize, Let its al - tar reach the skies.

core and just, In heav'n we place a man - ly trust, That truth and jus - tice may pre-vail, And ev - 'ry scheme of bond-age fail.

CHORUS
Firm, u - nit - ed let us be, Rallying round our Lib-er - ty! As a band of brothers joined, Peace and safe-ty we shall find.

3 Behold the chief who now commands,
Once more to serve his country stands,
The rock on which the storm will beat;
The rock on which the storm will beat;
But, armed in virtue, firm and true,
His hopes are fixed on heaven and you.
When hope was sinking in dismay,
When gloom obscured Columbia's day,
His steady mind from changes free,
Resolved on death or Liberty!—*Cho.*

Battle Hymn of the Republic.—*Concluded.*

4 He has sounded forth the trumpet that shall never call retreat;
He is sifting out the hearts of men before His judgment seat;
Oh, be swift, my soul, to answer Him! be jubilant, my feet!
Our God is marching on.—Cho.

5 In the beauty of the lilies, Christ was born across the sea,
With a glory in His bosom that transfigures you and me;
As He died to make men holy, let us die to make men free,
While God is marching on.—Cho.

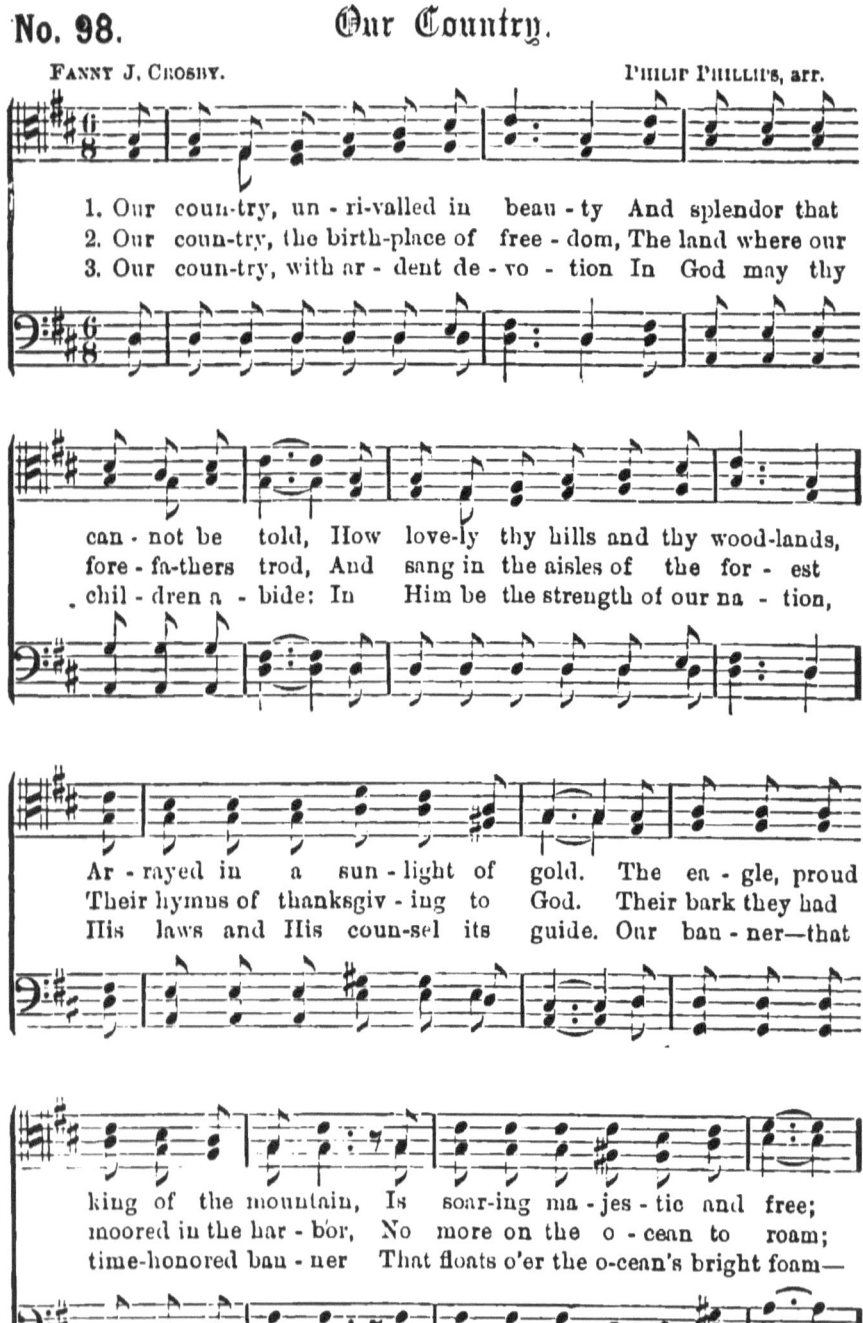

No. 100.   **Our Native Land.**

FANNY J. CROSBY.   German Air, arr.

1. With fil - ial love we cling to thee, Na-tive land, our na-tive land;
2. Thy fields are broad with plenty crowned, Na-tive land, our na - tive land;
3. Where first the stars of freedom rose, Na-tive land, our na - tive land;

The cradling place of lib - er - ty, Na-tive land, our na - tive land;
Thy state-ly trees with fruit abound, Na-tive land, our na - tive land;
Our veteran sires in peace re-pose, Na-tive land, our na - tive land;

No oth-er clime such deeds has done; No oth - er flag such fame has won;
Where giant rocks ma - jes - tic rise, The ea - gle soars to reach the skies;
Their precepts old, their watchful care, The smile, the song, the earnest pray'r,

No home like thine be-neath the sun; Na - tive land, our na - tive land.
'Tis thee we love, 'tis thee we prize; Na - tive land, our na-tive land.
Like fadeless gems their children wear; Na - tive land, our na-tive land.

Words and arr. Copyright, 1898, by The Biglow & Main Co.

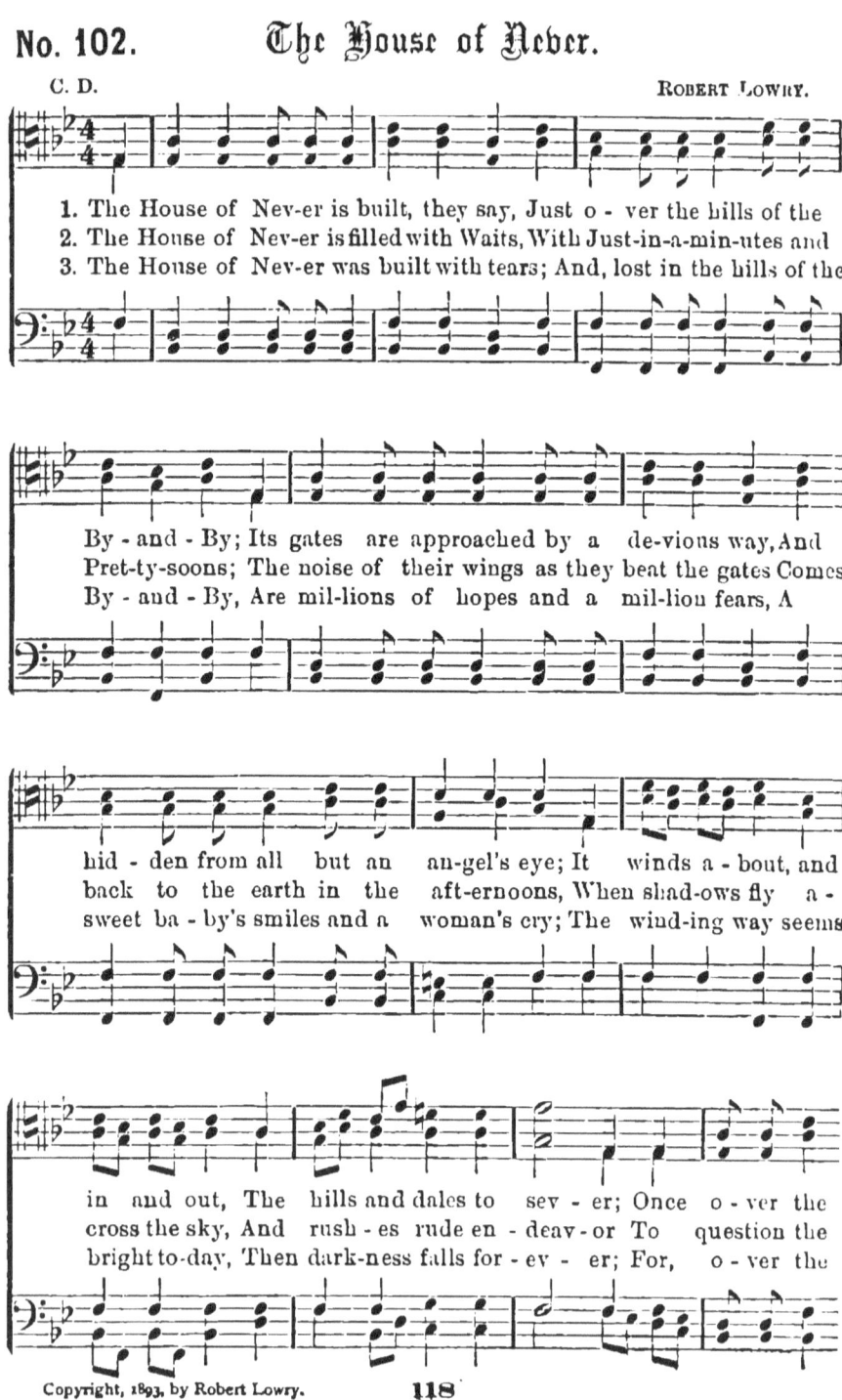

The House of Never.—*Concluded.*

hills of the By-and-By, And you're lost in the House of Nev-er.
hills of the By-and-By, As they ask for the House of Nev-er.
hills of the By-and-By, Sor - row waits in the House of Nev-er.

No. 103. God Bless Our Native Land.

JOHN S. DWIGHT. ROBERT LOWRY.

1. God bless our na - tive land; Firm may she ev - er stand,
2. For her our prayer shall rise To God a - bove the skies;

Thro' storm and night; When the wild tempests rave, Rul - er of
On Him we wait; Thou who art ev - er nigh, Guarding with

wind and wave, Do Thou our coun-try save By Thy great might.
watch - ful eye, To Thee a - loud we cry, God save the State!

Copyright, 1893, by The Biglow & Main Co.

No. 104. I Wandered by the Brookside.

RICHARD M. MILNES.   I. B. WOODBURY, arr. H. P. MAIN.

Melody, prominent.

pp

1. I wan-dered by the brook-side, I wan-dered by the mill, I could not hear the brook flow, The nois-y wheel was still; There was no hum of in-sect, No
2. I sat beneath the elm-tree, I watch'd the long, long shade, And as it grew still lon-ger I did not feel a-fraid; I list-en'd for a foot-fall,— I
3. He came not, ah! he came not, The night came on a-lone, The lit-tle stars sat dark-ly, Each on his gold-en throne; The eve-ning air pass'd by me, The

Tra la la la, la la la la, Tra la la la, la la la la, Tra la la la, la la la la, Tra la la la, la la la la,

Arr. Copyright, 1898, by The Biglow & Main Co.

No. 106. **There's Music in the Air.**

FANNY J. CROSBY.   GEO. F. ROOT.

1. There's mu-sic in the air When the ear-ly morn is nigh,
2. There's mu-sic in the air When the noon-tide's sultry beam
3. There's mu-sic in the air When the twilight's gen-tle sigh

And faint its blush is seen On the bright and laughing sky;
Re-flects a gold-en light In the dis-tant mountain stream;
Is lost in evening's breast, As its pen-sive beauties die;

Many a harp's ec-stat-ic sound, With its thrill of joy profound,
When beneath some grateful shade, Sorrow's ach-ing head is laid,
Then, O then, the loved ones gone, Wake the pure ce-les-tial song;

While we list en-chanted there, To the mu-sic in the air.
Sweet-ly to the spir-it there, Comes the mu-sic in the air.
An-gel voic-es greet us there, In the mu-sic in the air.

INDEX.

Titles in SMALL CAPITALS—*First lines in* Roman.

	NO.
AFTER THE DARKEST HOUR	36
"ALL'S CLEAR UP ALOFT"	33
AMERICA	93
Are you keeping close to Jesus	39
Are you shining for Jesus	71
AT EVENING TIME	40
At evening time may there be light	60
A young man stands at the parting	20

B

BATTLE HYMN OF THE REPUBLIC	97
BEYOND THE SMILING AND THE	65
BIRD WITH A BROKEN WING	53
BLUE GALILEE	62

C

Columbia, the gem of the ocean	96
COME, LOVE, HASTEN WITH ME	109
COME, SINNER, COME	87
COME UNTO ME	26
COMING HOME REJOICING	17
Coming out of darkness	17

D

DAY IS DYING IN THE WEST	91
DESCEND, O FLAME	51
DOWNWARD SINKS THE SETTING SUN	110

E

EVENING PRAYER	11
EVENING TIME	60

F

FLY TO THE REFUGE	10
FOR YOU AND FOR ME	49

G

GOD BLESS MY BOY	63
GOD BLESS OUR NATIVE LAND	103
GOD SAVE THE PEOPLE	7

	NO.
GOD SHALL WIPE AWAY ALL TEARS	79
GOOD-NIGHT, MY BROTHER	48
GRACE DIVINE	14
Great is the Lord who ruleth over	88

H

HAIL COLUMBIA	95
Hark! hark, my soul! angelic	51
HARK! THERE COMES A WHISPER	83
Have the millions been told	67
HE IS DESPISED	72
HERE AND THERE	85
Here, is the darkness, here, the toil	85
Holy Ghost, with light divine	76
HOME, SWEET HOME	108
Hope, fair and sweet, that on	50
HOW DEAR TO MY HEART	45
HOW LONG	46

I

I AM REDEEMED	18
I COULD NOT DO WITHOUT THEE	89
I HAVE ENOUGH	82
I heard the trailing garments of	99
I HEARD THE VOICE OF JESUS SAY	29
I, John, saw the Holy City	79
I LIFT MY HEART TO THEE	23
I walked through the woodland	53
I WANDERED BY THE BROOKSIDE	104
I was wandering, sad and weary	55
IMPATIENT HEART, BE STILL	78
In the land of strangers	15
Into the dark unknown	4
IS IT NOTHING TO YOU	43

J

JESUS, SAVIOUR, PILOT ME	28
JUST FOR TO-DAY	3

K

| KEEPING CLOSE TO JESUS | 39 |

INDEX.—*Concluded.*

L	NO.
Last Hope	76
Late, late, so late	59
Lead, kindly Light	12
Lead On	4
Look away to Jesus	64
Lord, for to-morrow and its needs	3

M

'Mid pleasures and palaces	108
Mine eyes have seen the glory	97
My Country, 'tis of thee	93
My Faith looks up to Thee	68
My weary soul a rest hath found	52

N

Night	99

O

O I am a merry sailor lad	101
O I Love to Talk with Jesus	81
O Mother dear, Jerusalem	32
O my Redeemer	27
O Paradise	16
O Rock of Ages	52
O say, can you see, by the dawn's	94
O the Beautiful Hills of the	61
O Zion, Lovely Zion	9
One Sweetly Solemn Thought	77
Only a Little While	19
On the Resurrection morning	74
Onward and Upward	69
Onward, Onward	13
Onward, Soldiers, Onward	58
Our Country	98
Our Native Land	100
Out of the darkness into the	70

P

Pilgrims of Night	51
Praise and Magnify our King	88
Praise to the Holy One	1
Press toward the Mark	31

R

Red, White and Blue	96
Remember me, O Mighty One	38
Resting just a Moment	5
Resurrection Morn	74
Ring out the word from Christ	31
Rock of Ages	44
Room for All	22

S

Saved by Grace	86
Saviour, the day is declining	24
Seek Ye the Lord	70
Send the Word	67

	NO.
Shining for Jesus	71
Show Your Colors	30
Sleep on, beloved, sleep, and	56
Softly and tenderly, Jesus is calling	49
Some day the silver cord will	86
Sound the Gospel Trumpet	66
Spread the Sails	25
Stand for Christ, your Leader	8
Star of the Morning	55
Stars of the Summer Night	105
Steal Away	57
Stealing from the world away	11
Sweet and Low	107
Sweet Peace	37

T

The Beautiful Hills	61
The Christian's Good-night	56
The Christian's Hope	50
The House of Never	102
The King of Love	21
The Lord hath pardoned all my	14
The Lord is my Shepherd	92
The Merry Sailor Lads	101
The Parting of the Ways	10
The Sands of Time are Sinking	42
The Shepherd True	55
The Star-Spangled Banner	94
The Tide is Flowing Out	73
The weary hours like shadows	46
There comes to my heart one sweet	37
There is work that we can do	75
There may be stormy days	89
There's Music in the Air	106
There's room at the feet of the	22
Though your Sins be as Scarlet	90
Thy Sins are Forgiven thee	84
'Tis Harvest-tide	6
Too Late	59

U

Under His Wings	2

W

Welcome, Wanderer, Welcome	15
We would see Jesus	34
What a Friend Thou art to Me	27
When pearly moonbeams	62
When shining stars their vigils	63
When storms around are sweeping	18
When wilt Thou save the people	7
Where God and the Angels are	80
Where will you spend Eternity	41
While Jesus whispers to you	87
Whisper a Message	24
Who are These	47
While the Years are Rolling by	75
With filial love we cling to thee	100

www.ingramcontent.com/pod-product-compliance
Lightning Source LLC
Chambersburg PA
CBHW020112170426
43199CB00009B/500